THE PORTABLE FEBRUARY

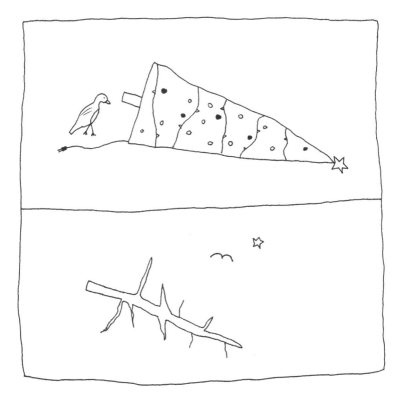

Drag City — Chicago

Second Printing, July 2020
Library of Congress control number: 2009926203
ISBN: 978-0-9820480-1-6
www.dragcity.com
DC386

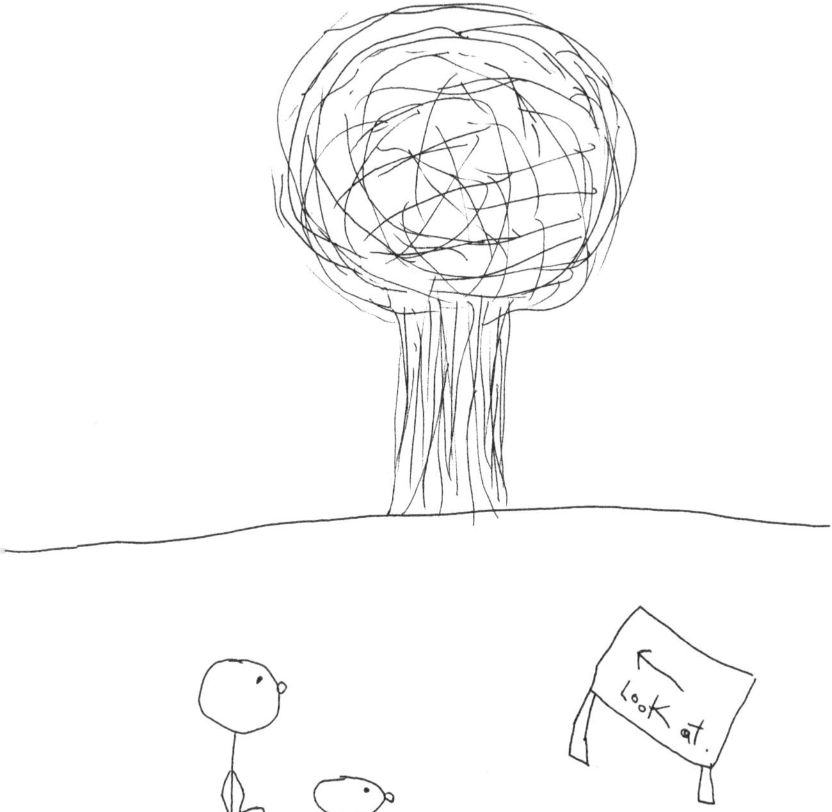
Look at.

Premise? I got premise.

The Rookie

Character Ark

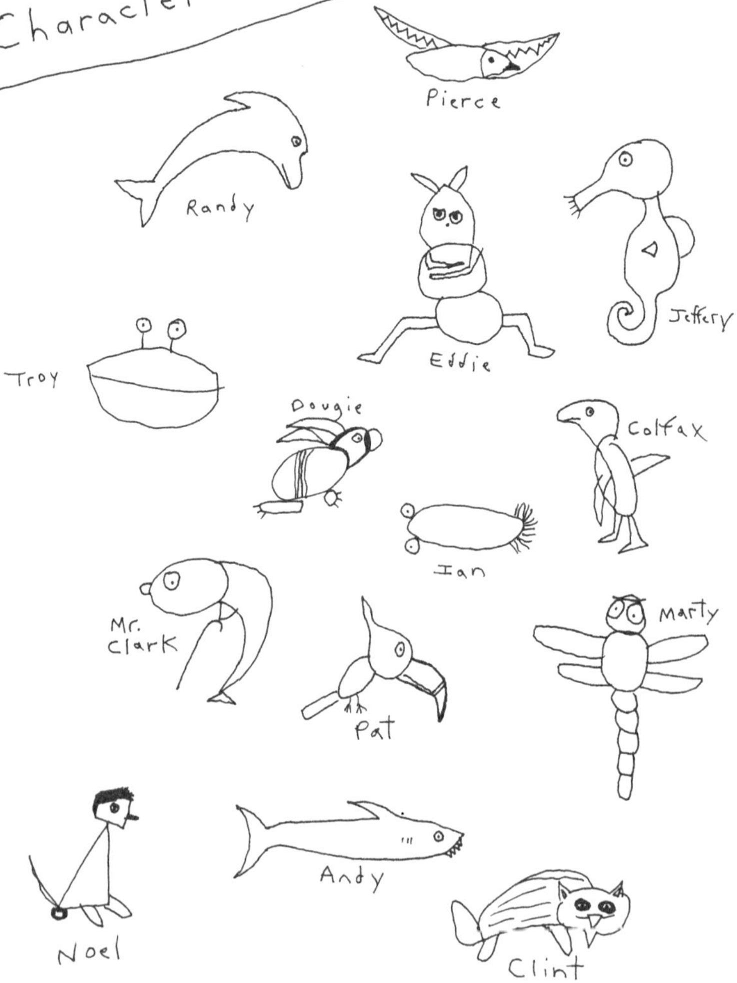

Pierce
Randy
Eddie
Jeffery
Troy
Dougie
Colfax
Ian
Mr. Clark
Pat
Marty
Noel
Andy
Clint

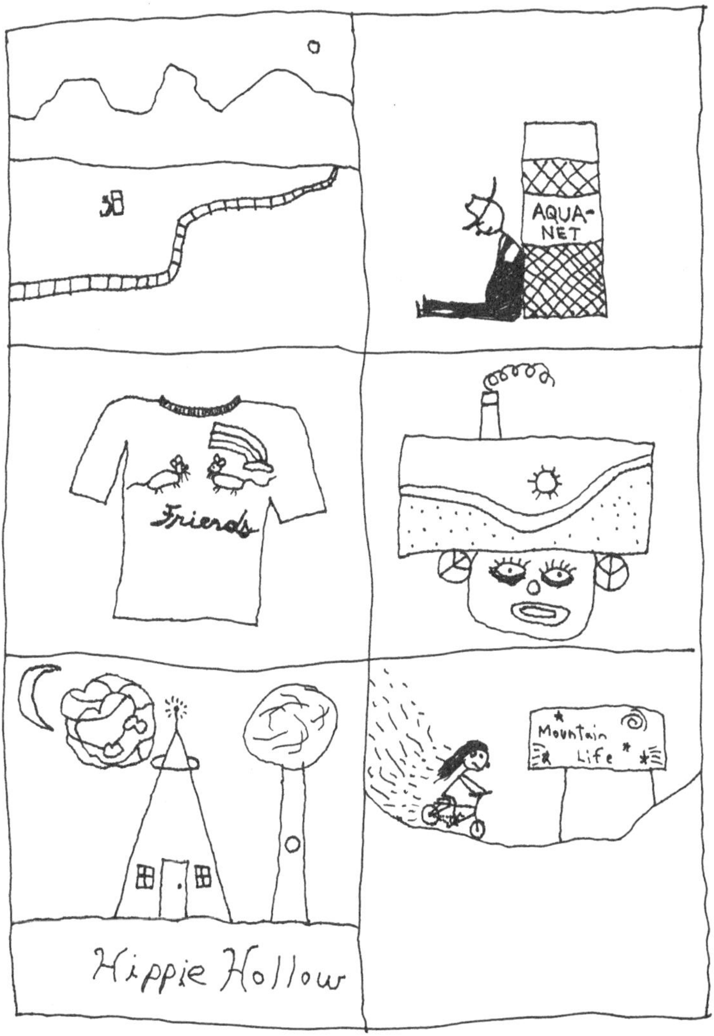
AQUA-
NET
Friends
Mountain
Life
Hippie Hollow

Wild celery.

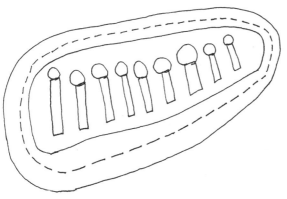

country road

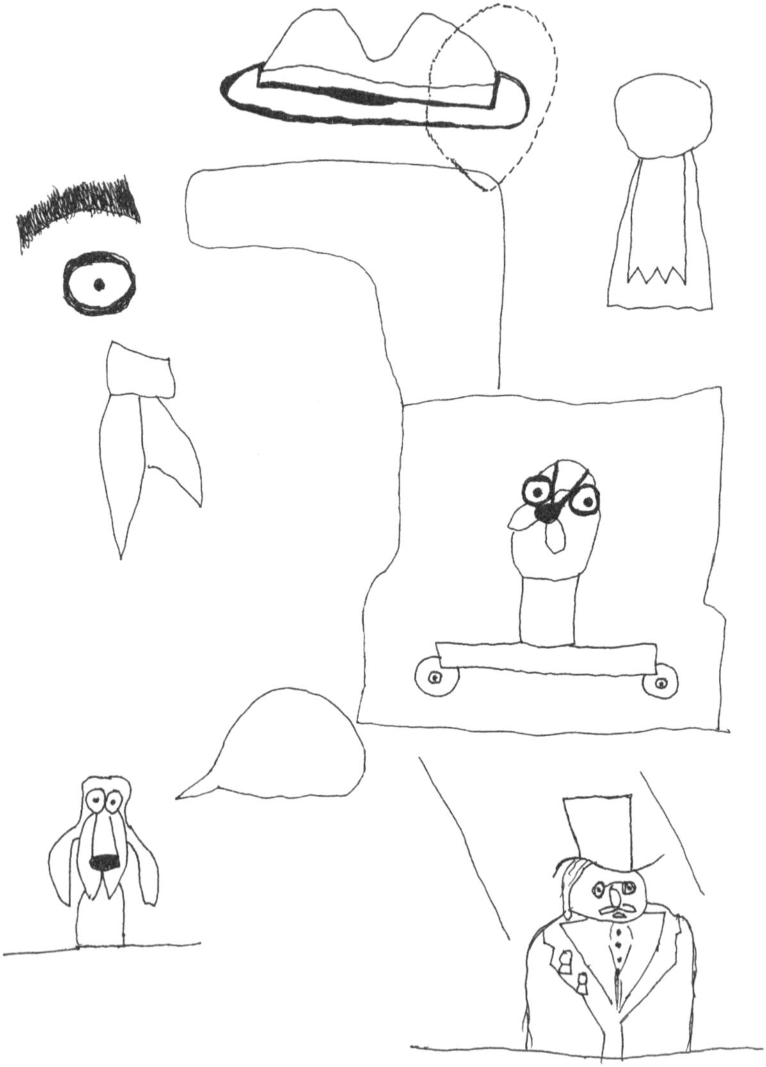

THE WORLD WE HAD

"We" stands for "warn everybody"

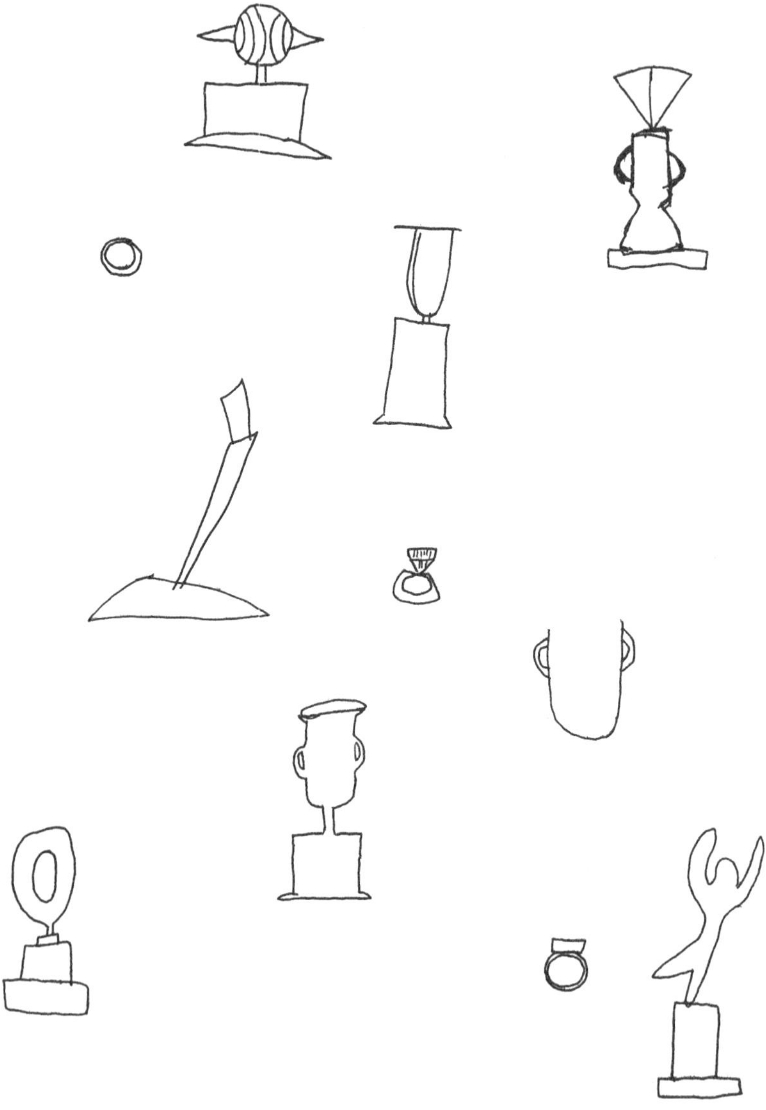

RINGS + TROPHIES

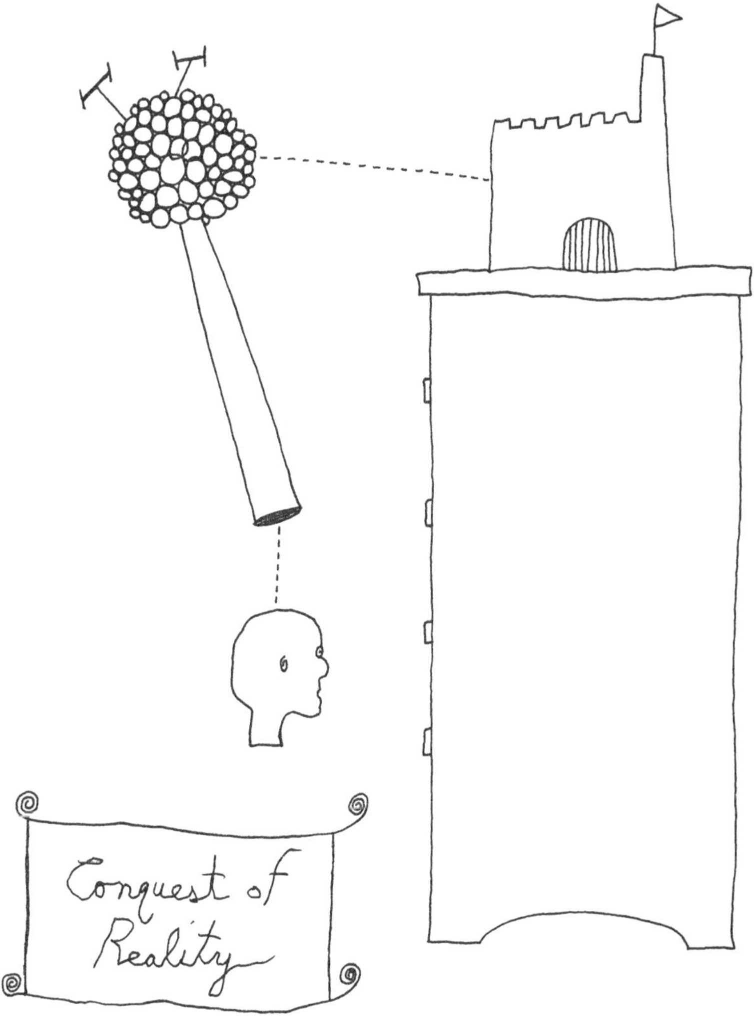
Conquest of Reality

"You don't have to believe in magic
to believe what I believe."

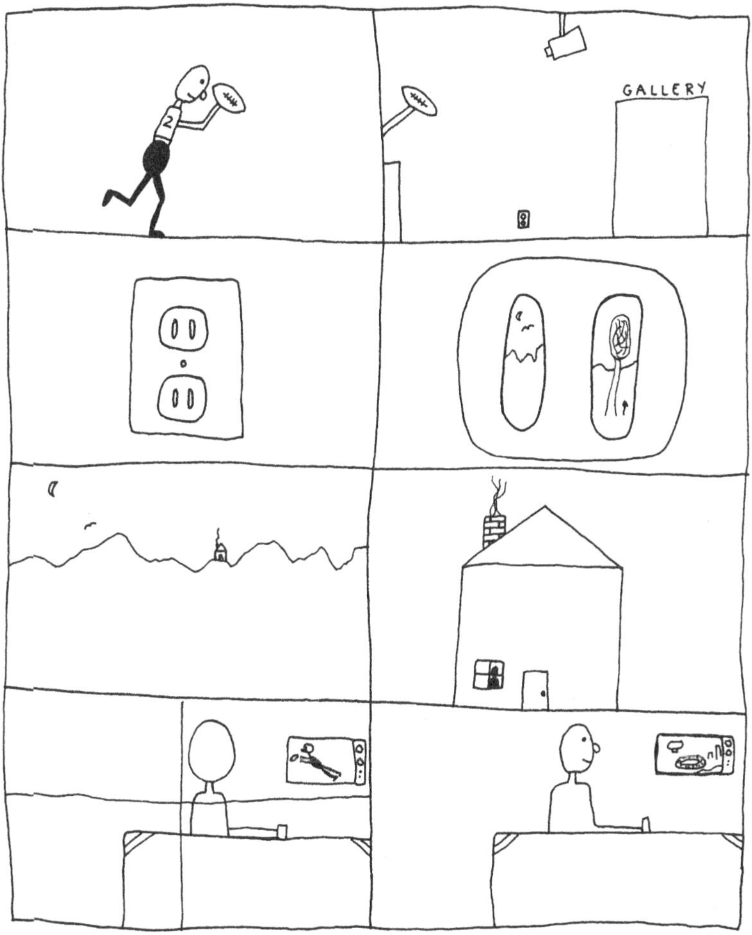
GALLERY

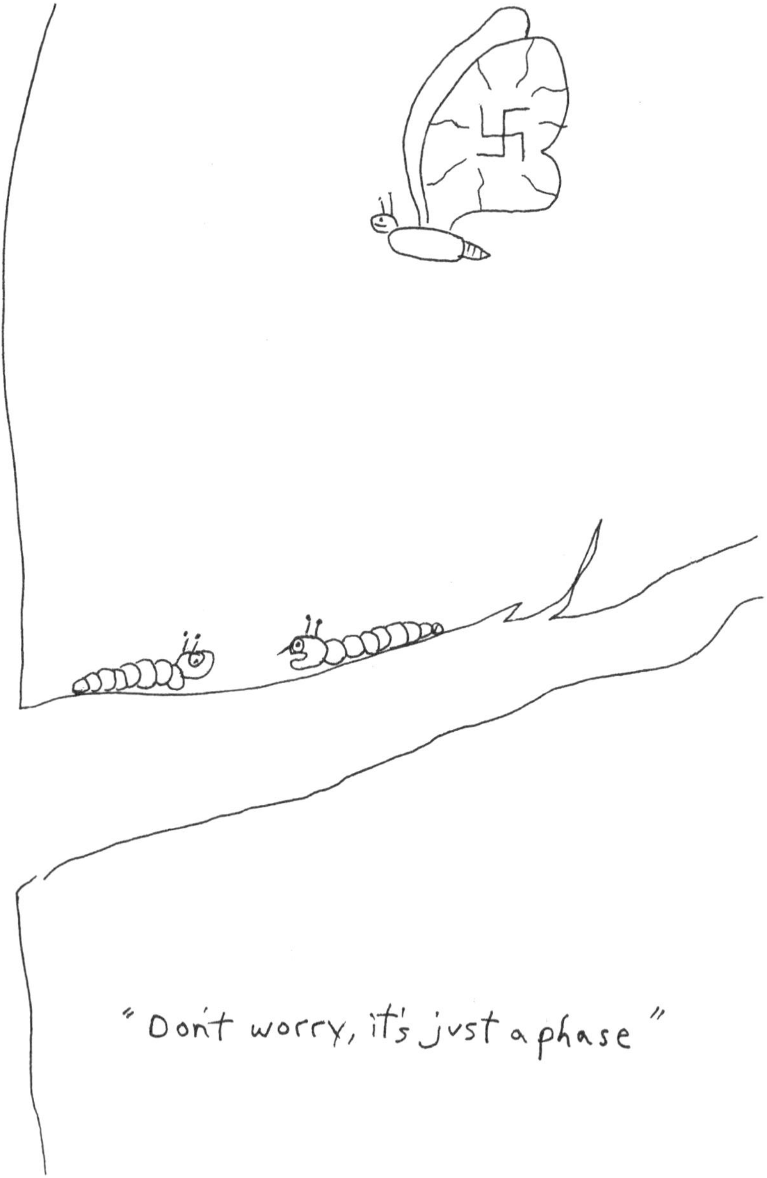

"Don't worry, it's just a phase"

Sea-Nerd

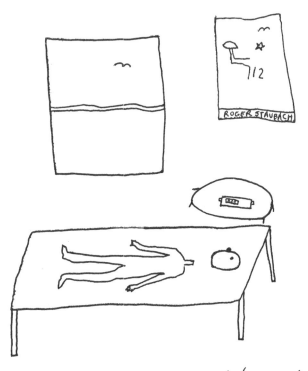

I lay in bed & listened to my clock radio.
They played a song called "Sara"
  every night. The lyrics went "drowning
  in a sea of love, where everyone would
  love to drown." It seemed evil,
    for someone to want to drown.

I can't feel my legs

INTEERESTING
interesting
interesting
interesting
interesting
interesting
interesting
interesting
interesting
interesting
interesting

Interesting Tree

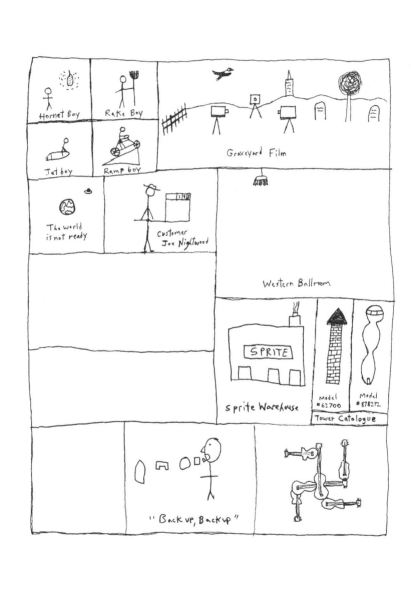

Hornet Boy

Rake Boy

Jet boy

Ramp boy

Graveyard Film

The world is not ready

Customer
Joe Nightwood

Western Ballroom

SPRITE

Sprite Warehouse

Model
#62700

Model
#878212

Tower Catalogue

" Back up, Back up "

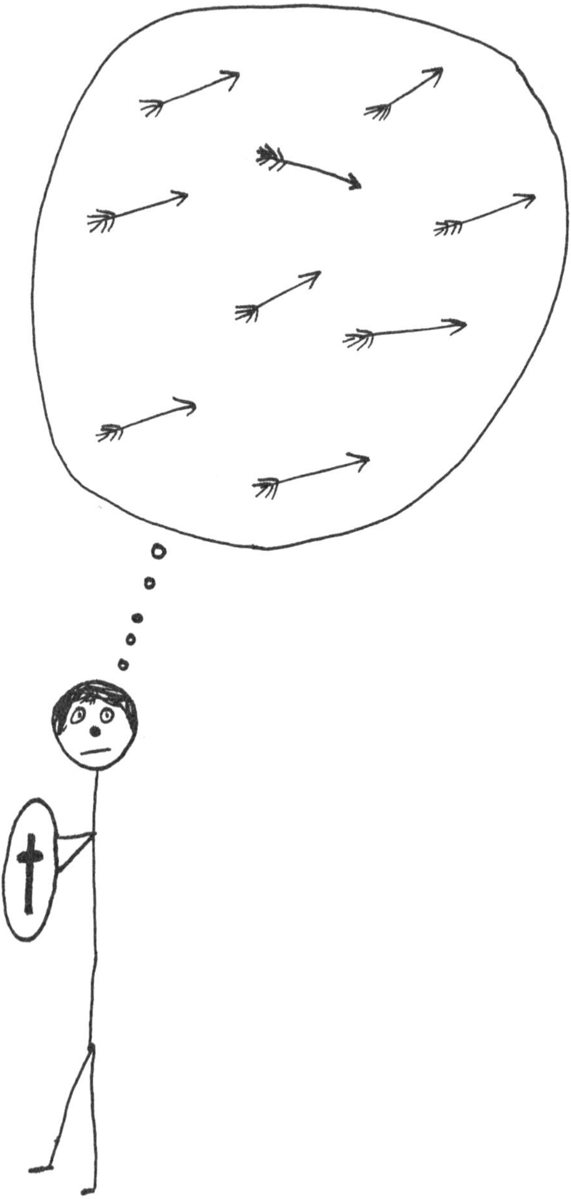

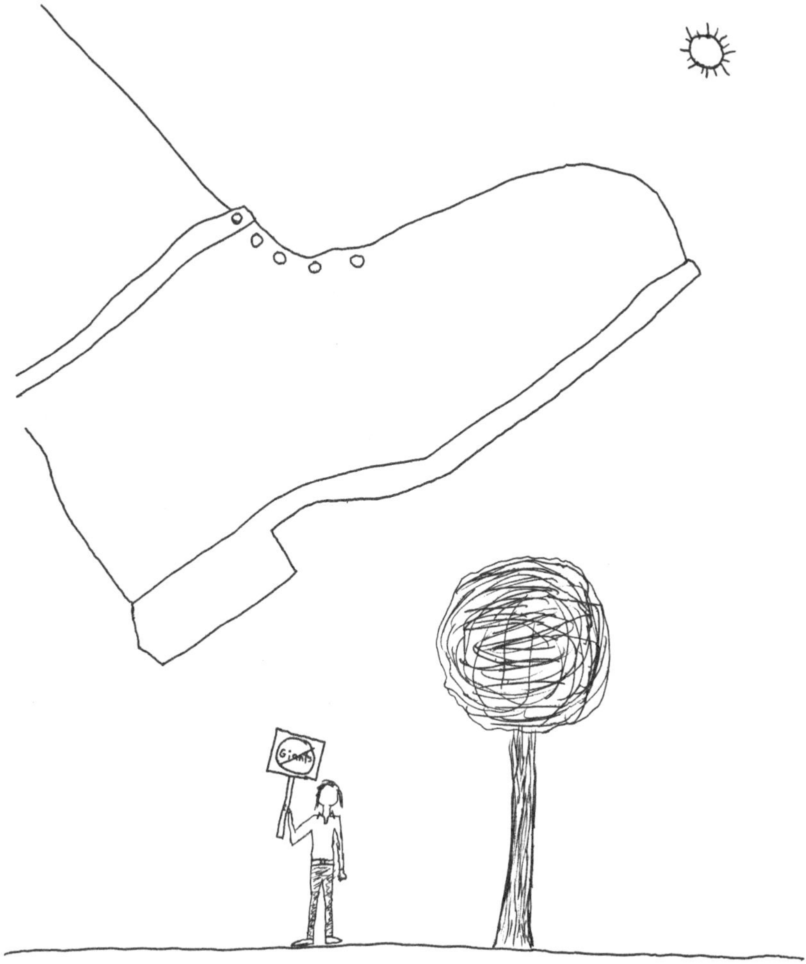
Giants

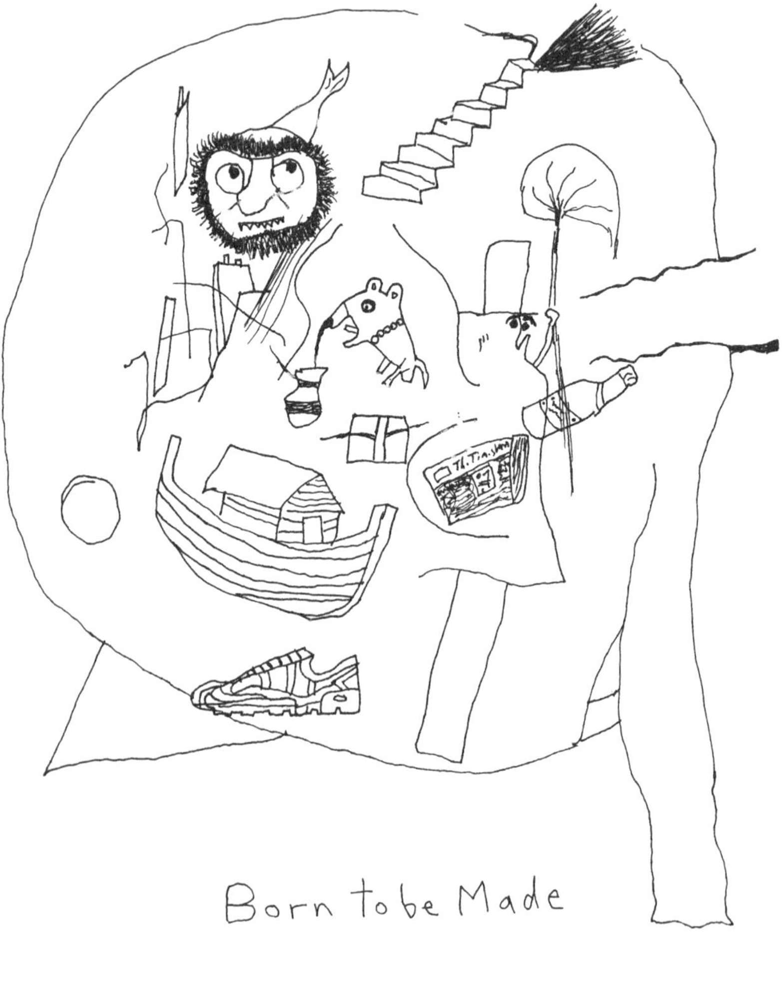

Born to be Made

Daytime Television.

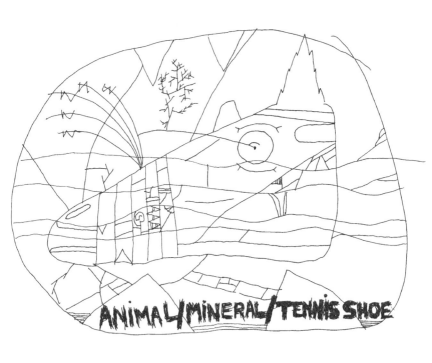

ANIMAL/MINERAL/TENNIS SHOE

Double Darkness
on the Adolescent Trail

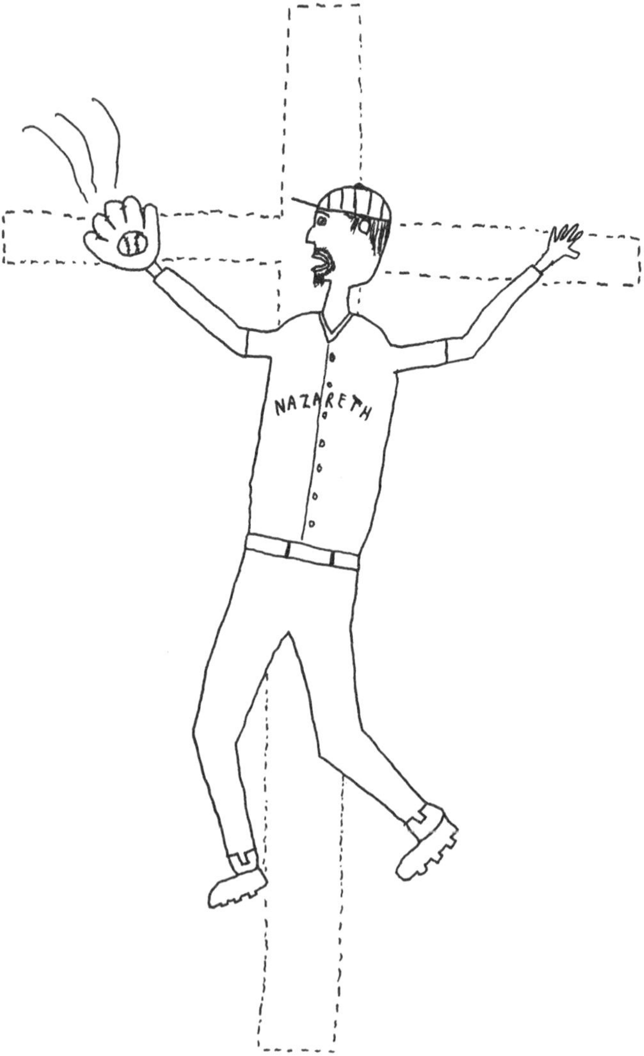
NAZARETH

Castration Eyes

Psycho-Social Interiors

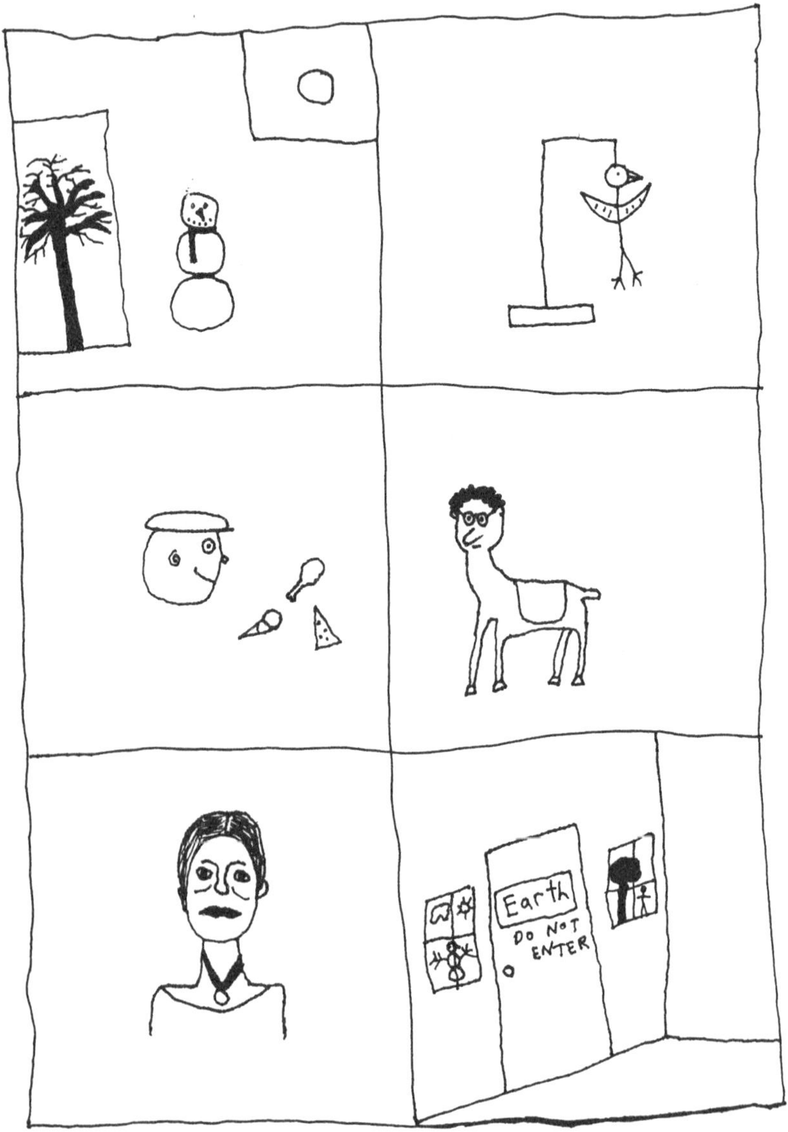

Earth
DO NOT ENTER

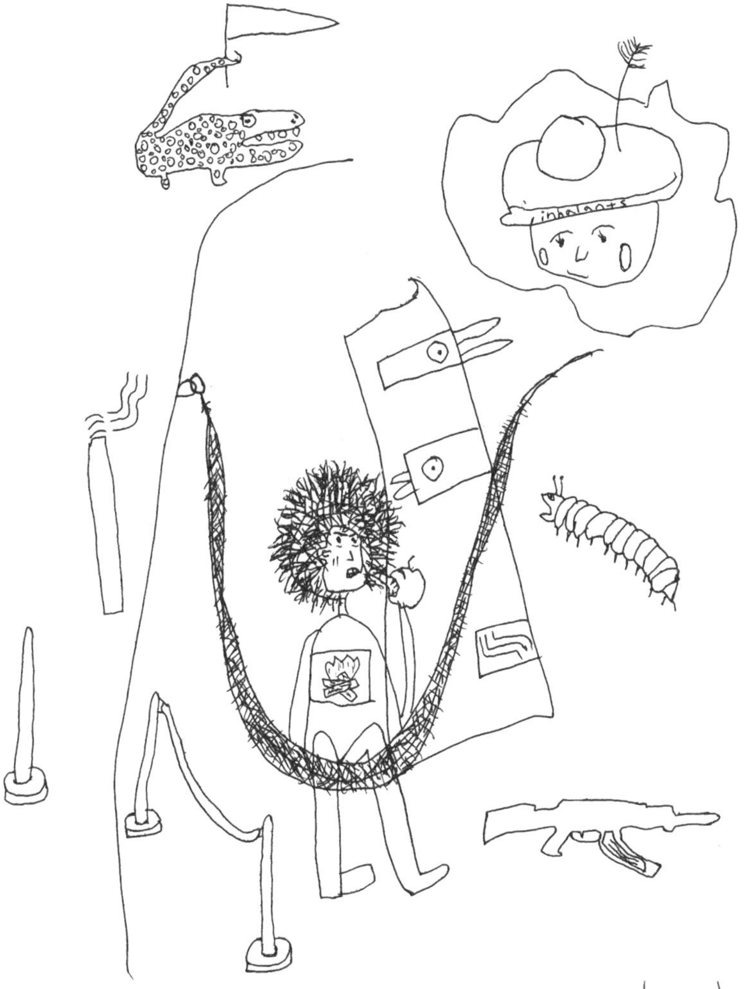
inhalants

the [redacted] grandson.

"Don't go old-fashioned on me now, Brian."

Be Your Own Kin

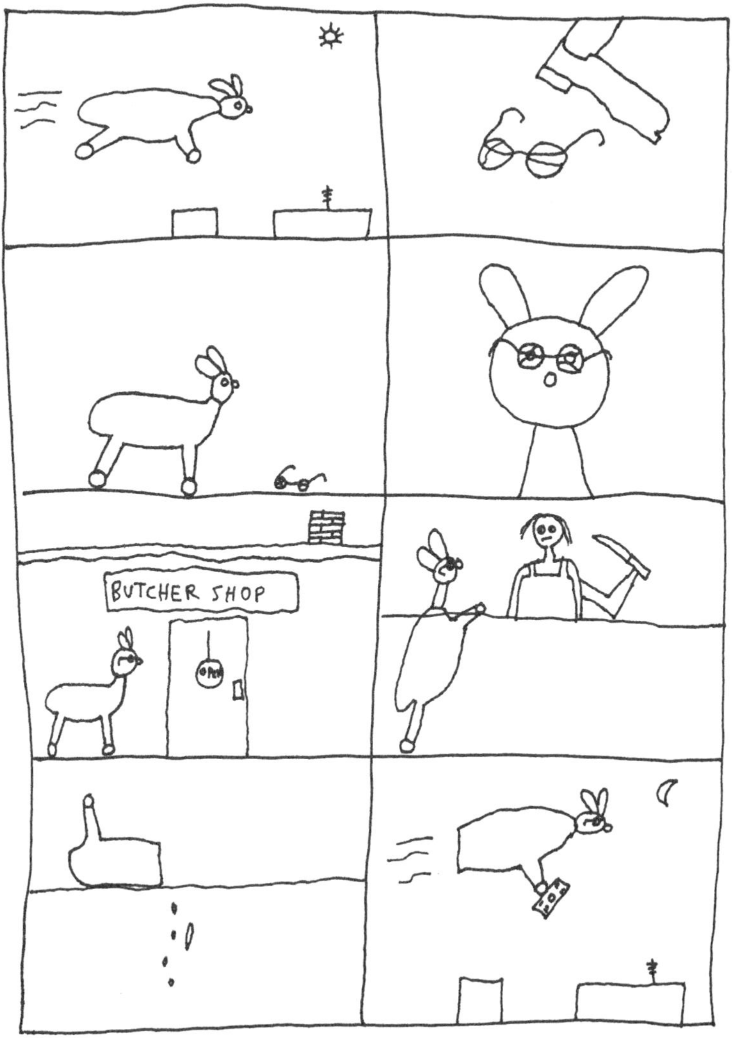
BUTCHER SHOP
OPEN

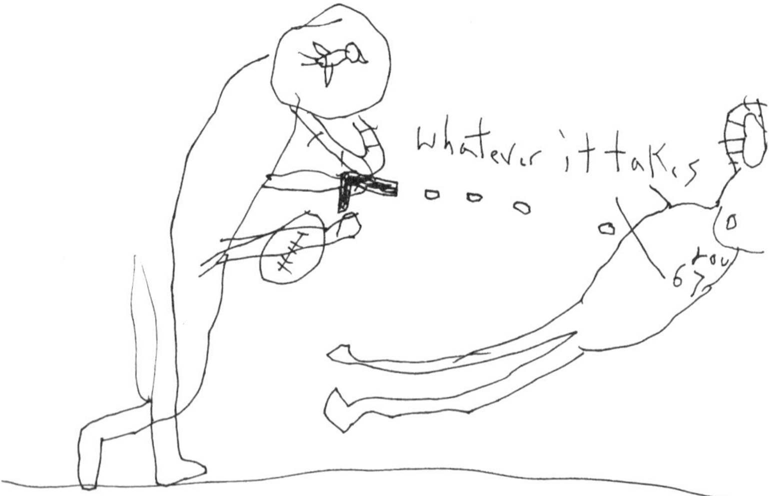
whatever it takes
you

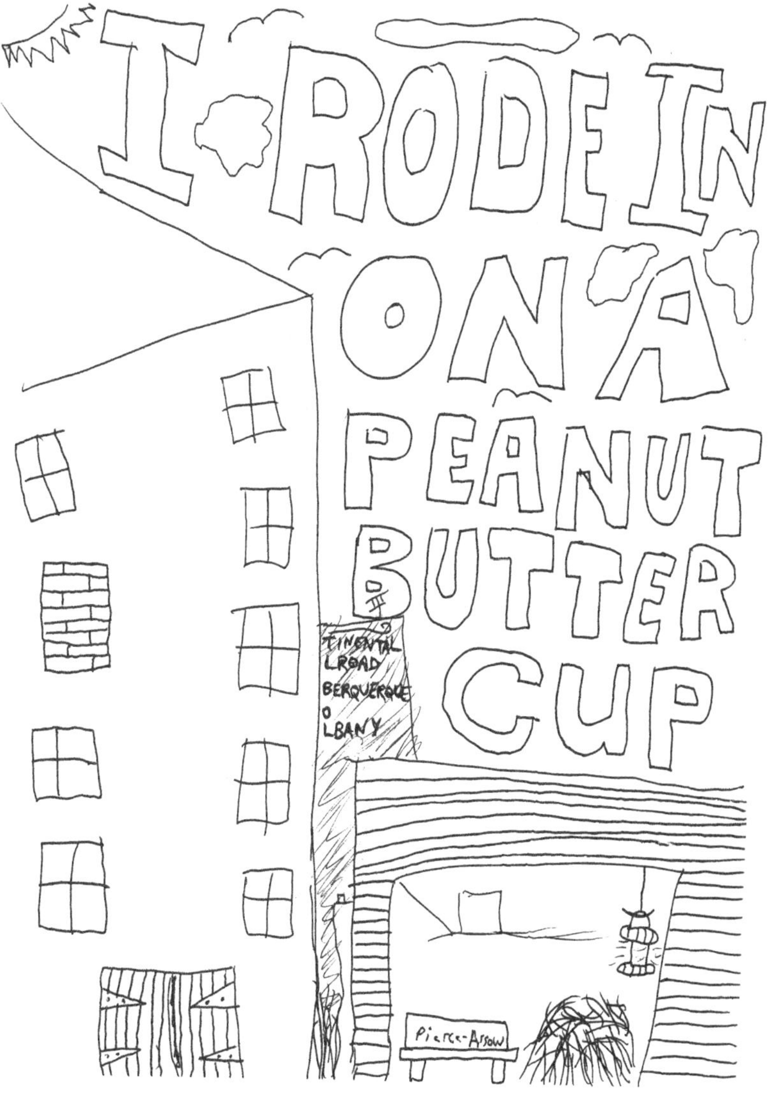
I RODE IN ON A PEANUT BUTTER CUP
TINENTAL
LROAD
BERQUERQUE
O
LBANY
Pierce-Arrow

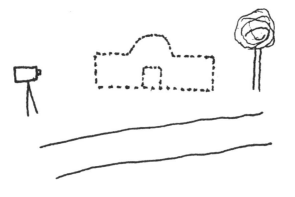

proposed mansion

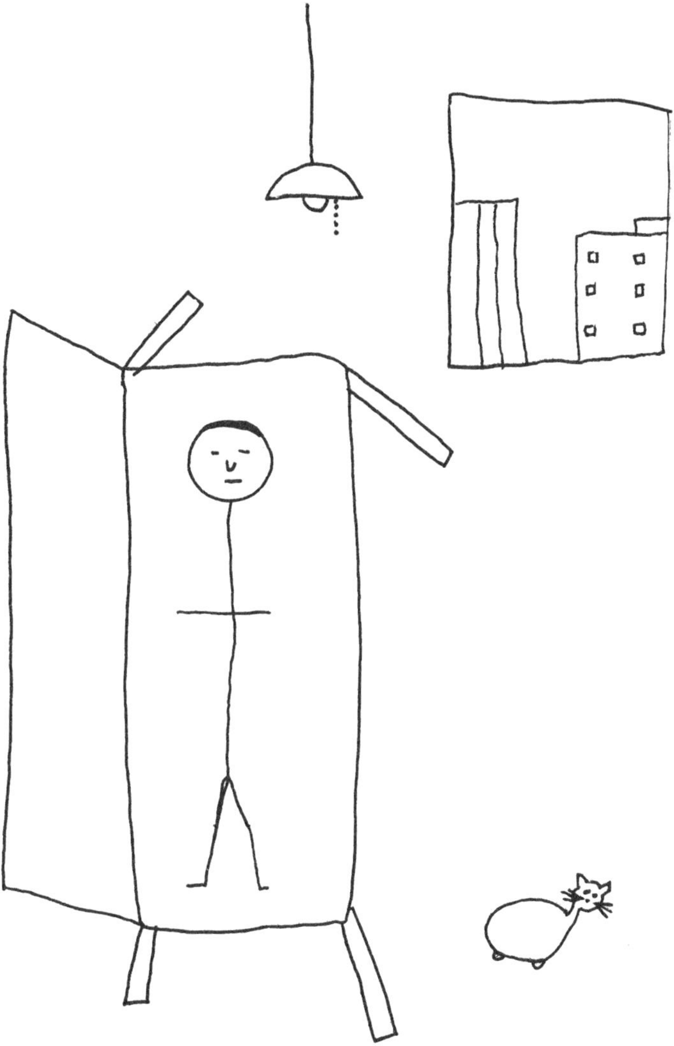

Napoleon in Memphis

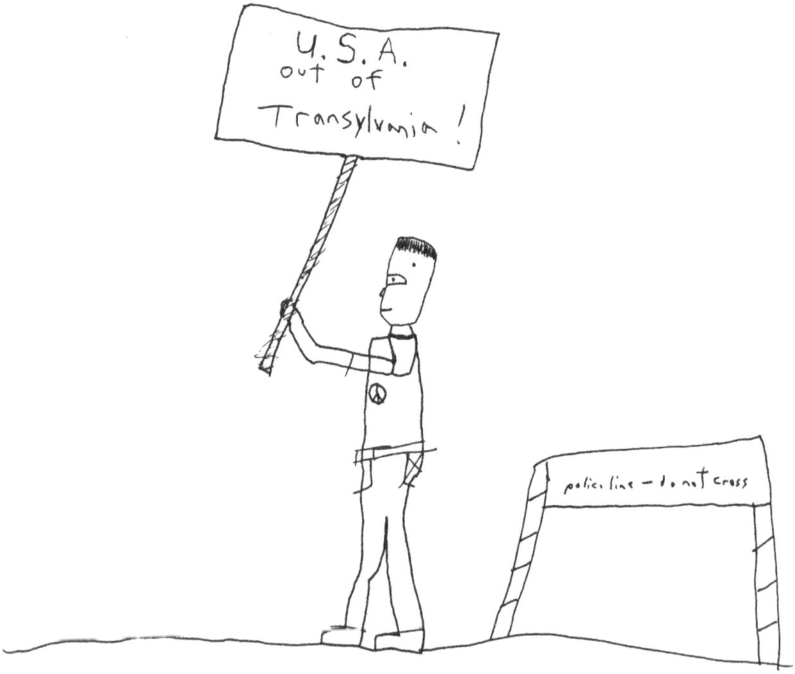
U.S.A.
out of
Transylvania!
police line – do not cross

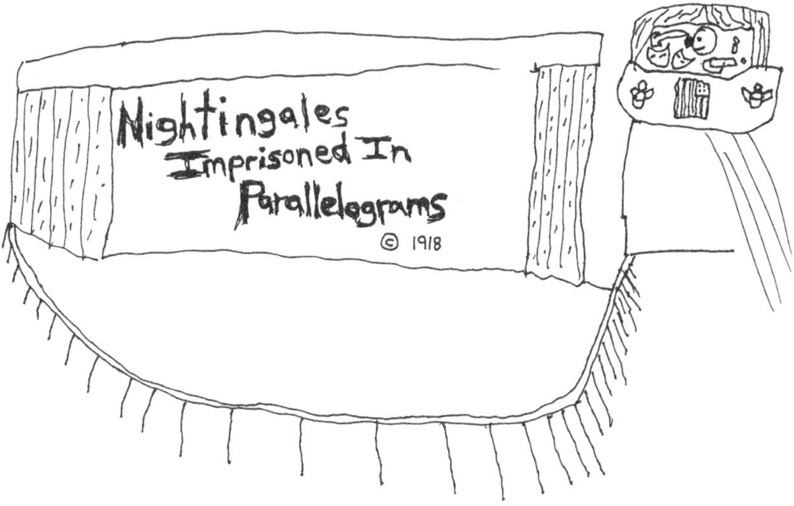
Nightingales
Imprisoned In
Parallelograms
© 1918

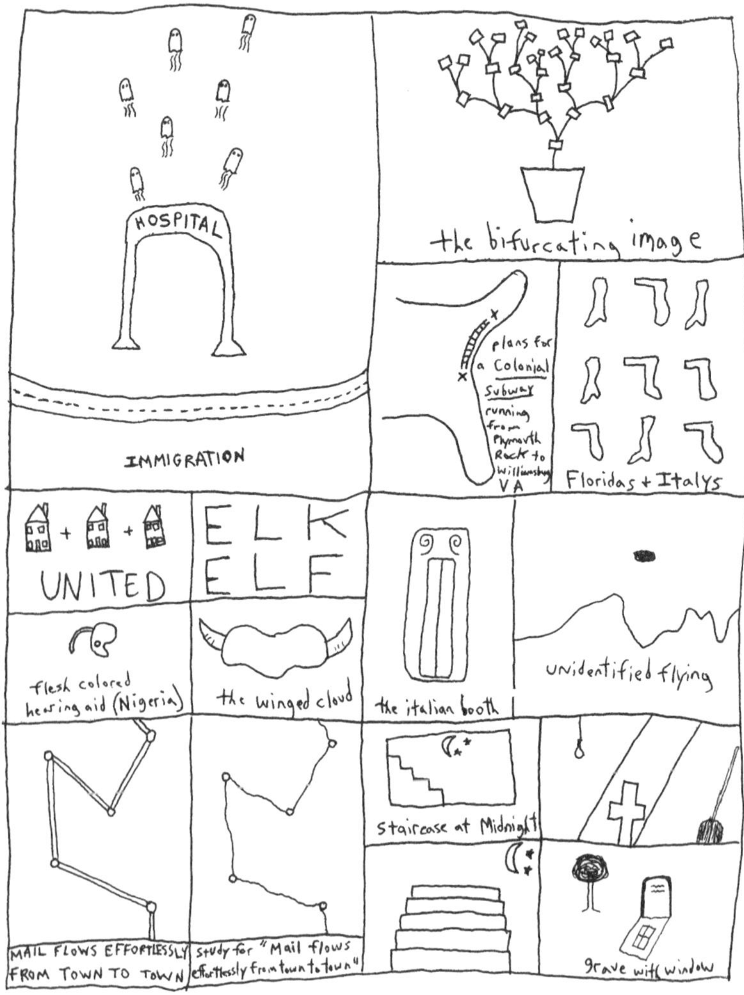
HOSPITAL
IMMIGRATION
the bifurcating image
plans for a Colonial Subway running from Plymouth Rock to Williamsburg VA
Floridas + Italys
UNITED
ELK
ELF
flesh colored hearing aid (Nigeria)
the winged cloud
the italian booth
unidentified flying
Staircase at Midnight
MAIL FLOWS EFFORTLESSLY FROM TOWN TO TOWN
study for "Mail flows effortlessly from town to town"
grave with window

five   cents

pasture on the back of a nickel

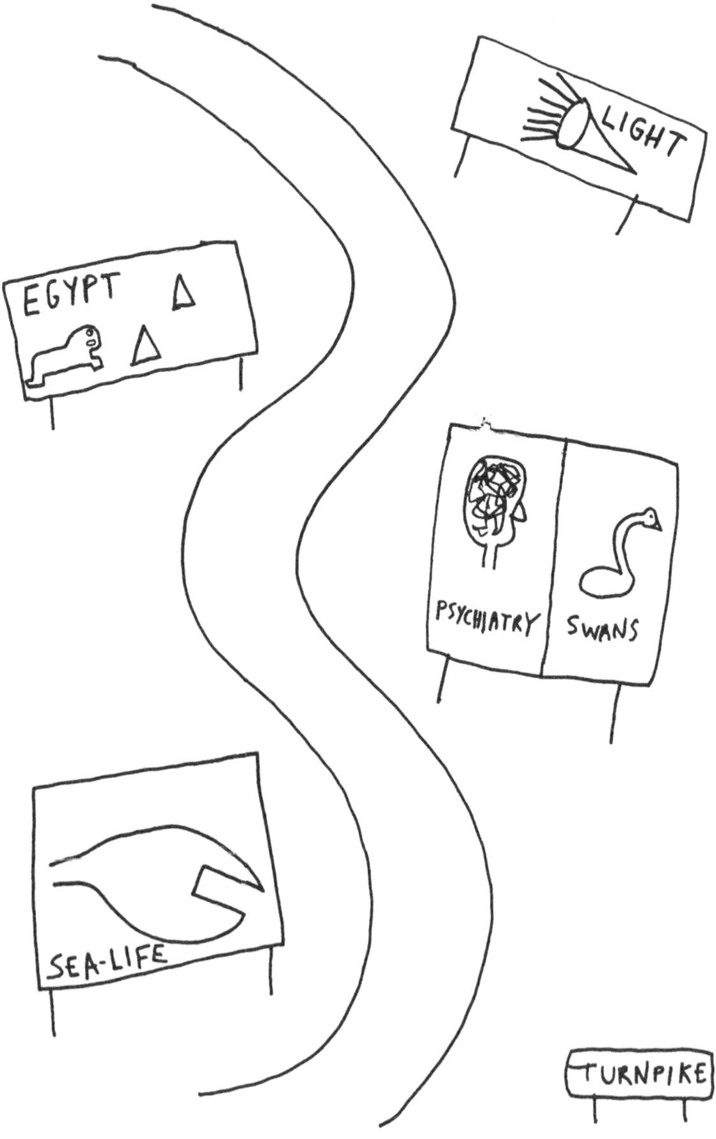
LIGHT
EGYPT
PSYCHIATRY
SWANS
SEA-LIFE
TURNPIKE

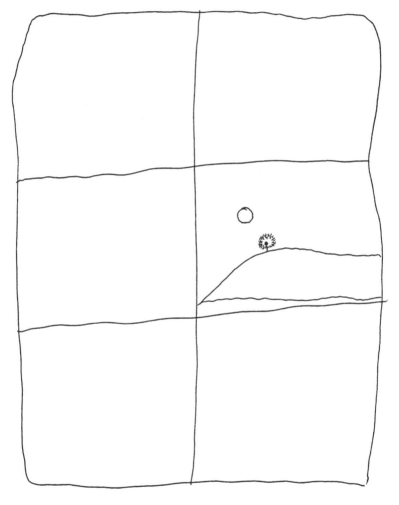

one long lost folk melody

Charles Guiteau waits for Garfield

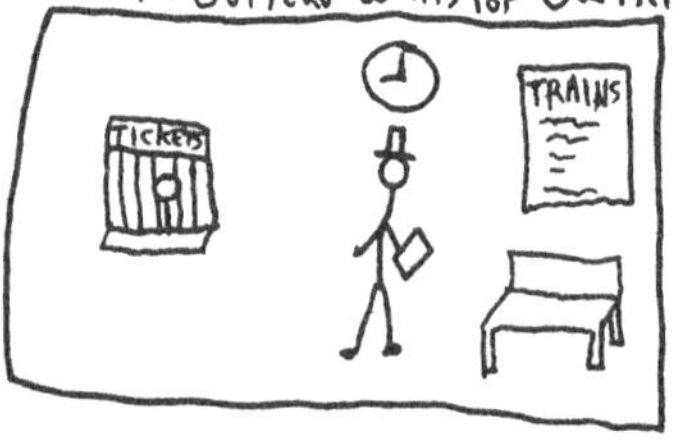
TICKETS
TRAINS

Detail of Firing Squad

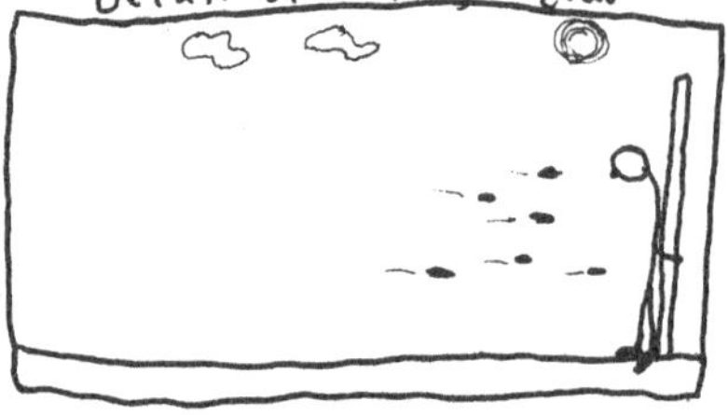

Assasin on the Rooftops

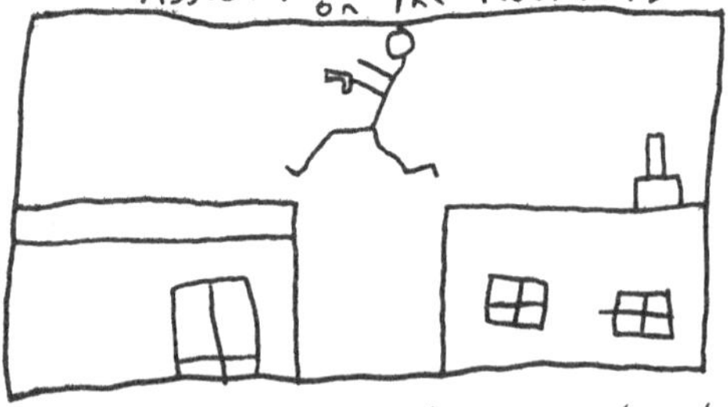

Execution Landscape

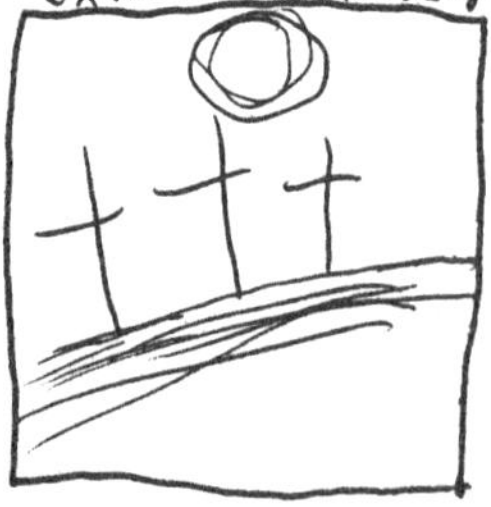

Bullet shot on empty plain, fading

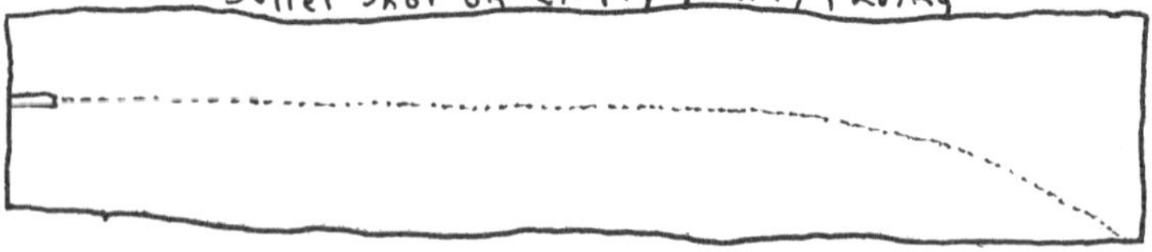

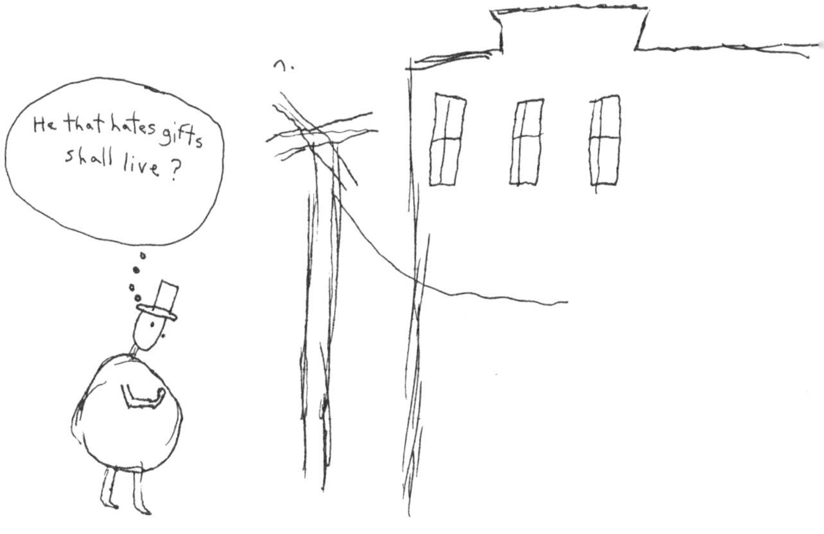
He that hates gifts shall live ?

"Are Yez All Looking!?"

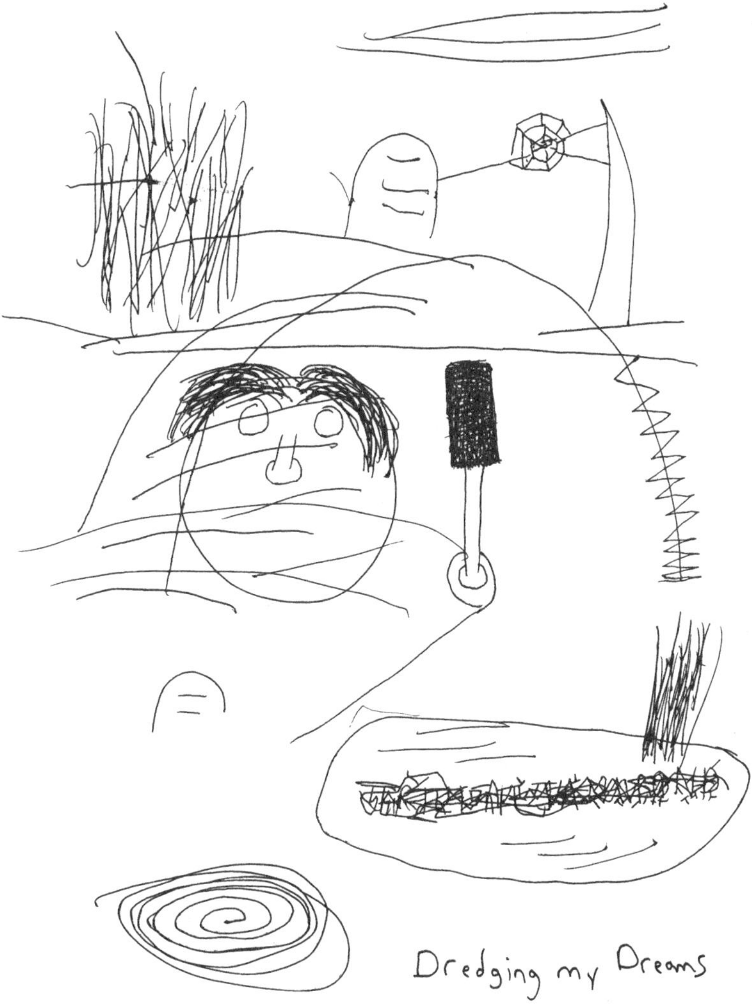

Dredging my Dreams

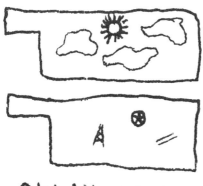

OKLAHOMA +
THE SKY OVER OKLAHOMA

WHITE
CARTOON
VOTERS.

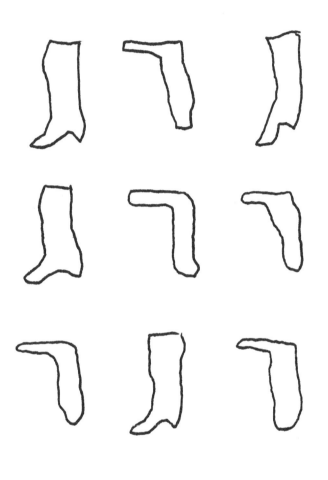

Floridas & Italys

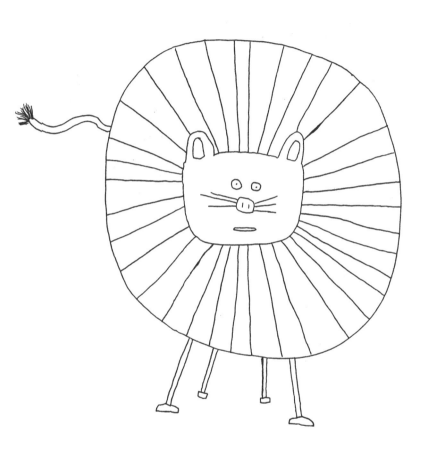

Iowa Lion

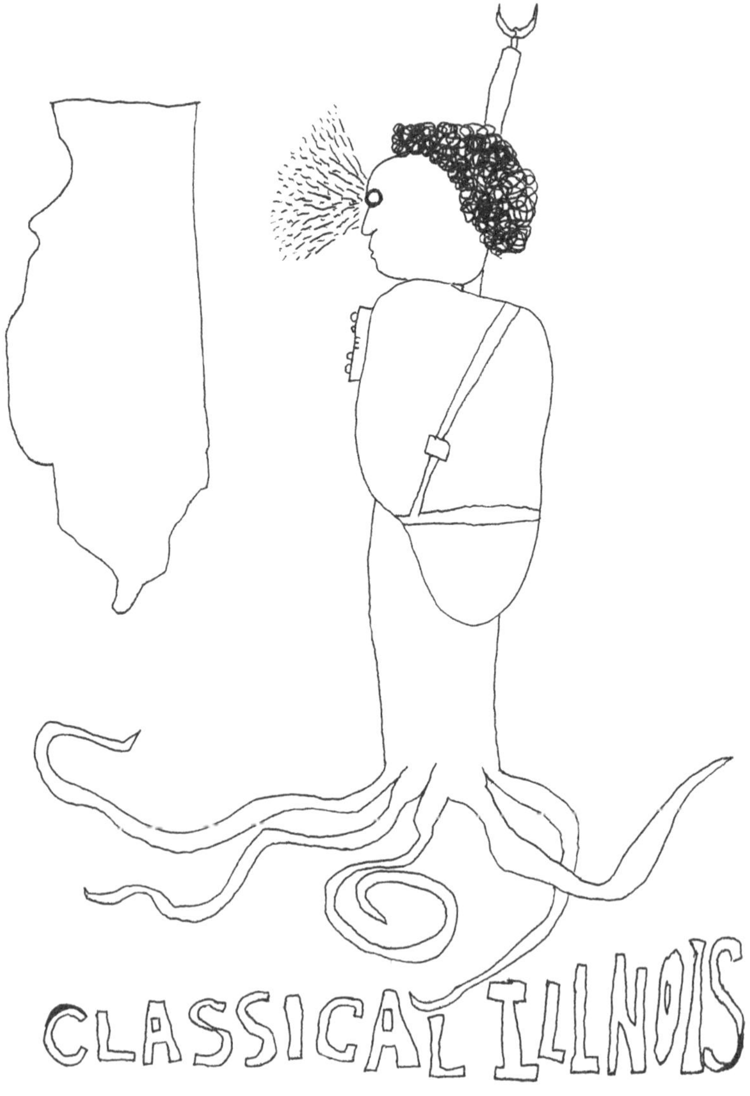
CLASSICAL ILLNOIS

A Place in New Jersey

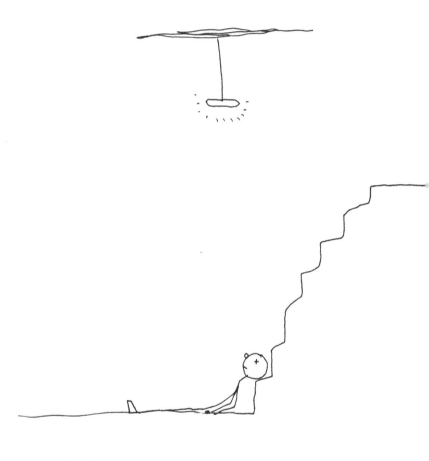

New Wave Bedrooms

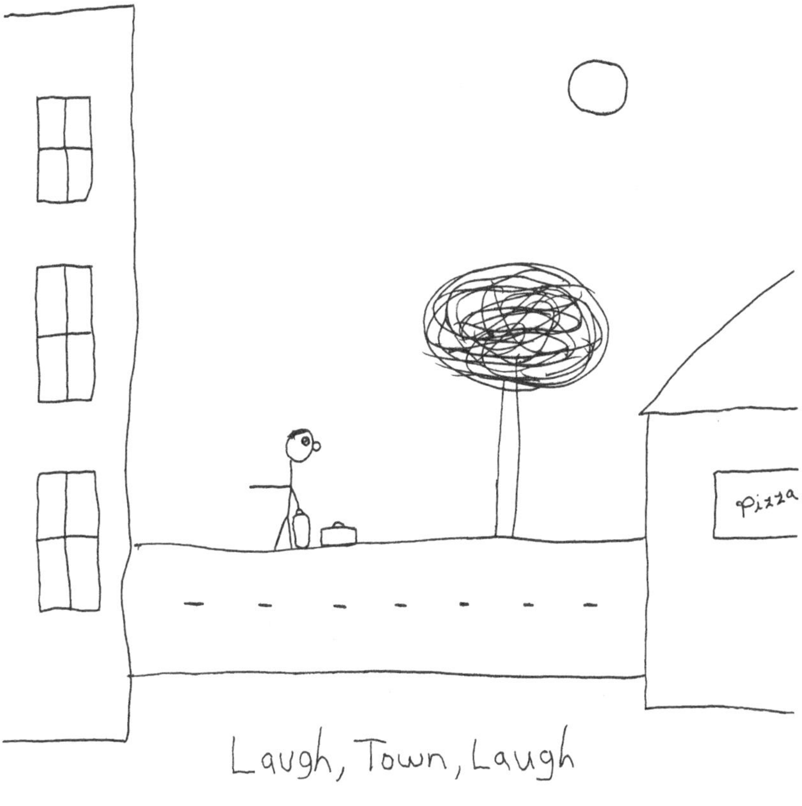
pizza

Laugh, Town, Laugh

Motion Pasture Theater

The Spring Break Hitlers

'Til Death Do Us Laugh

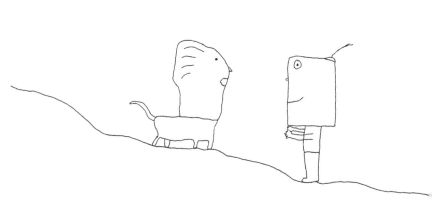

PARKING STORY

by M.T. Lott

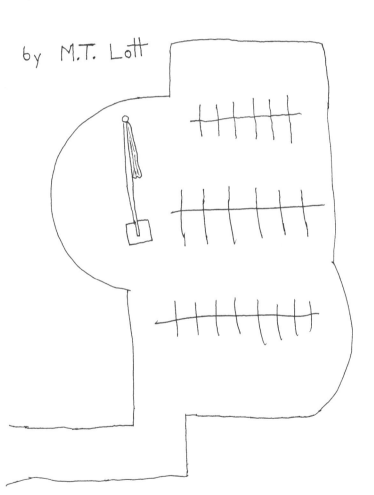

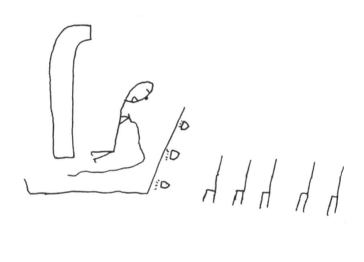

The Soul and its Shtick

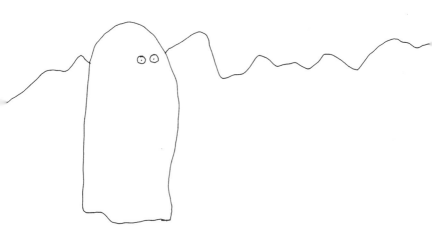

Death in the mountains

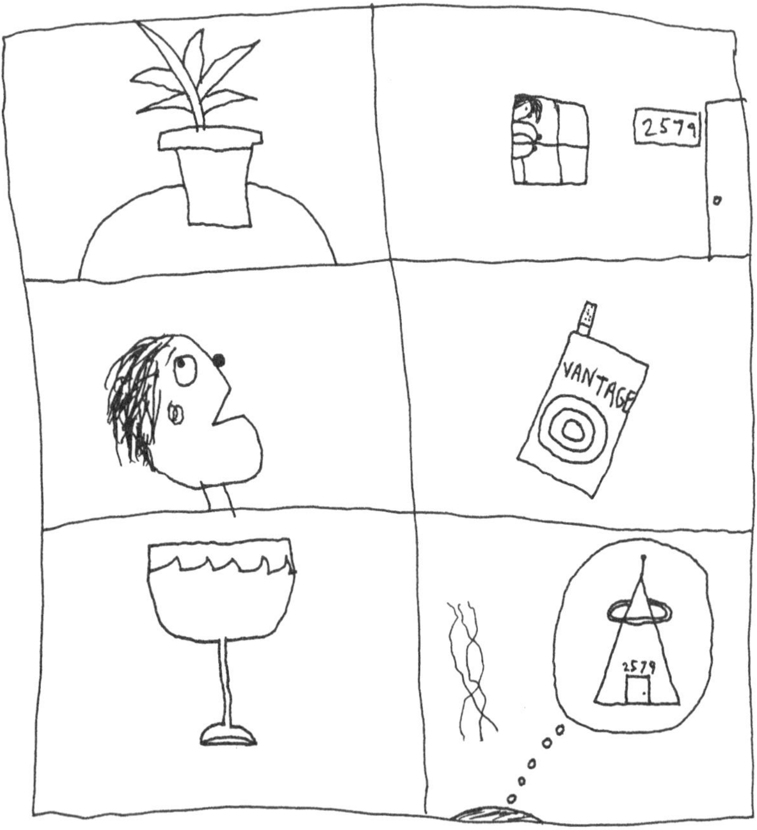
2579
VANTAGE
2579

Peak Velocity Banjo

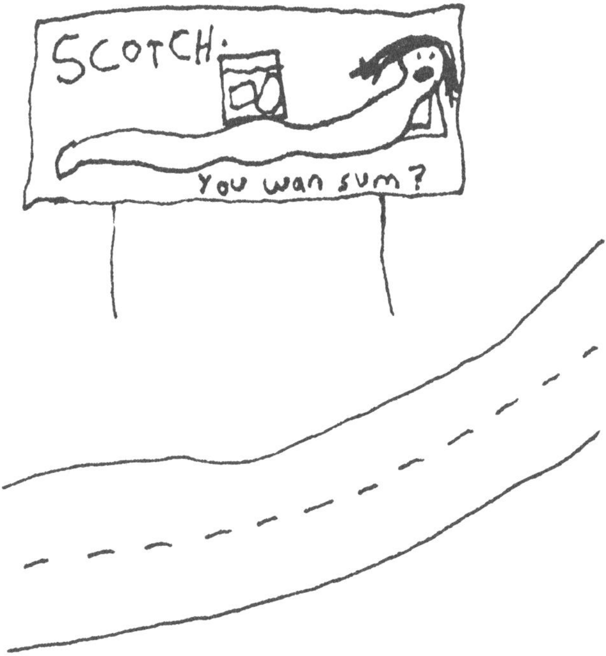
SCOTCH
You wan sum?

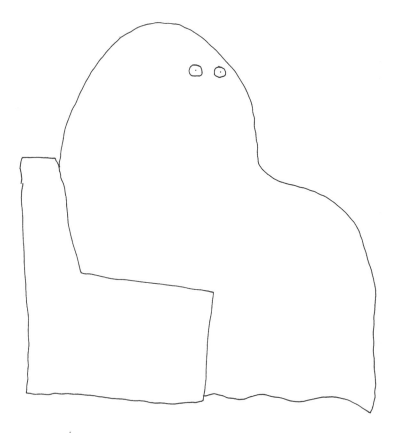

Death just sitting around with no one to Kill.

Taverns of the Sub-Neocortex

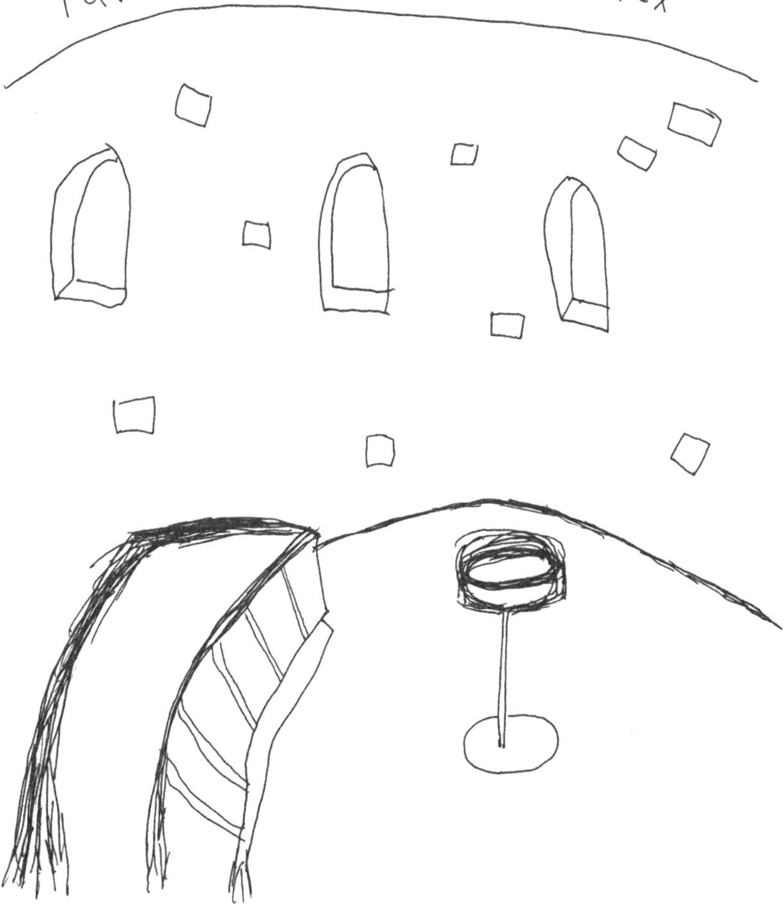

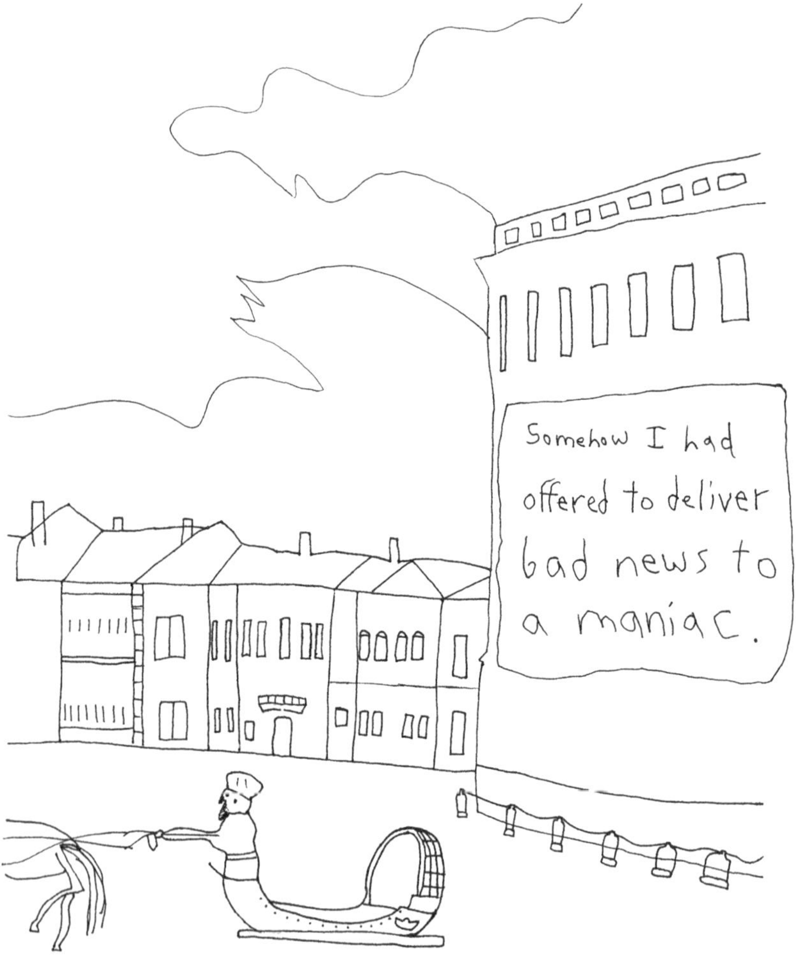
Somehow I had offered to deliver bad news to a maniac.

Bobcat, Chili, and Diamonds

If you were New Wave
in Cincinatti in 1983,
I probably haunted
your spare time occasionally.

"Once you dry off sir, I'll take you
right in to see the president."

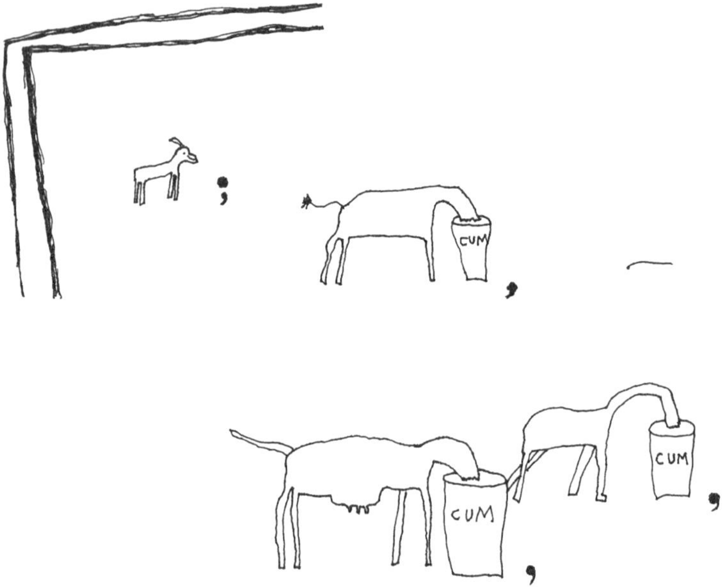
CUM
CUM
CUM

"The Intern"

O'ciety

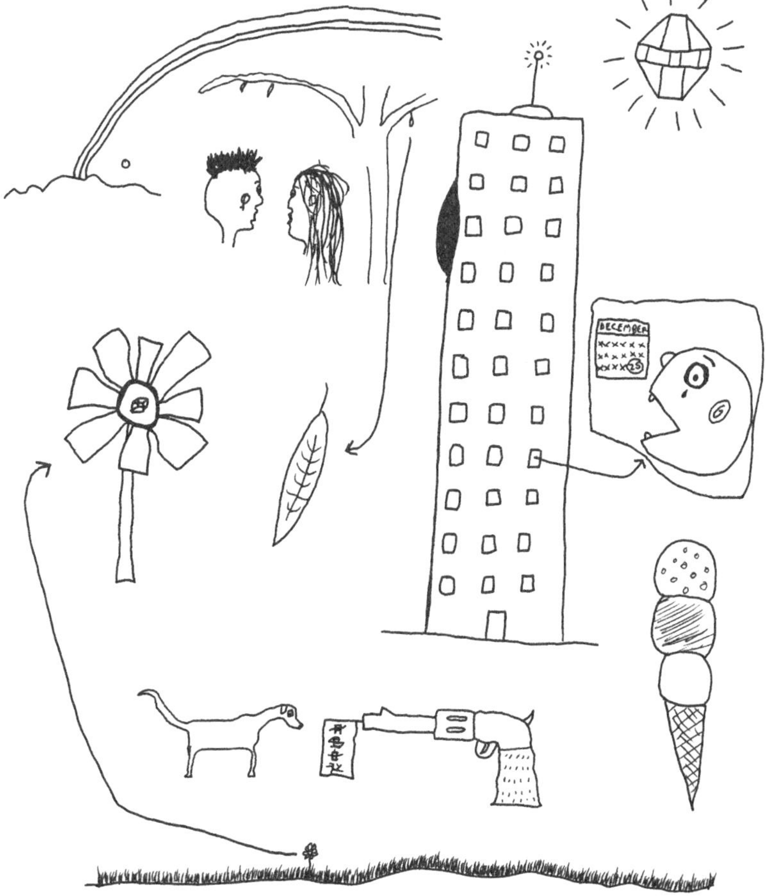
DECEMBER
25

Memo to the Pioneers

Irrational 15th Century Battle Scenes

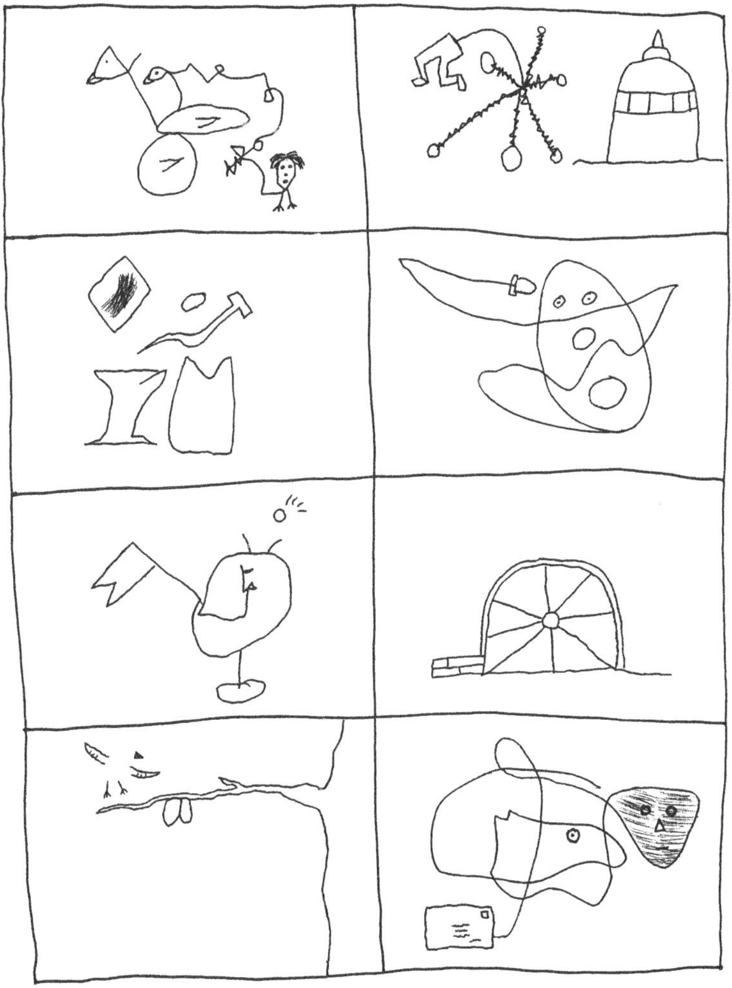

The Gift Connection

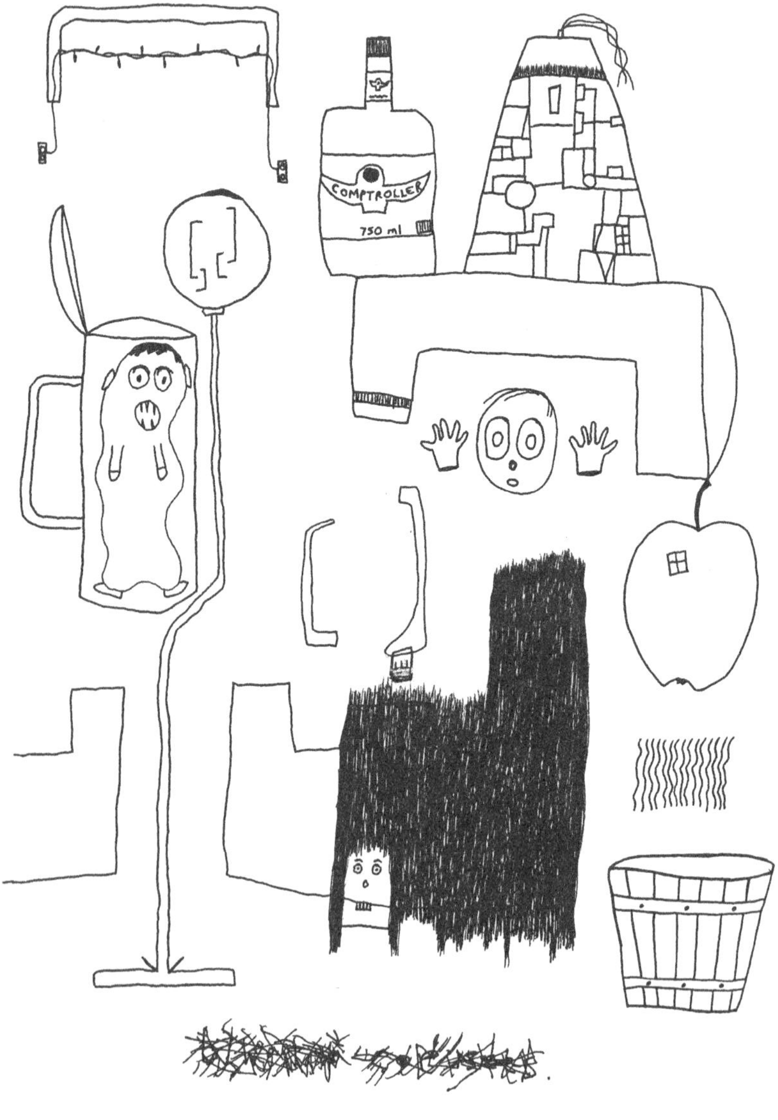
COMPTROLLER
750 ml

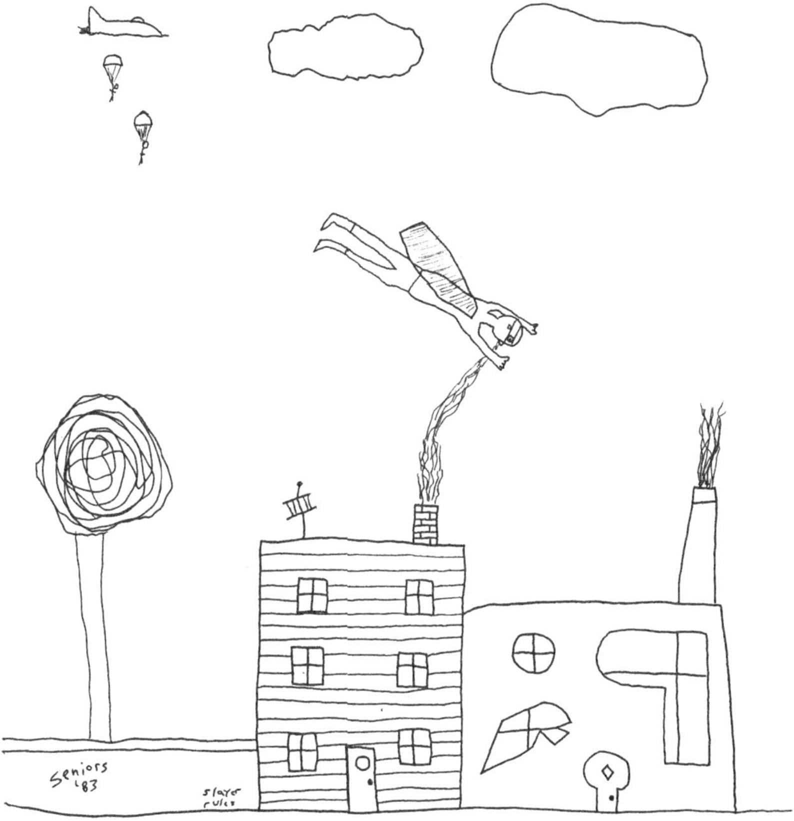
seniors '83
slayer rules

Cruising the Metropolitan Airshed

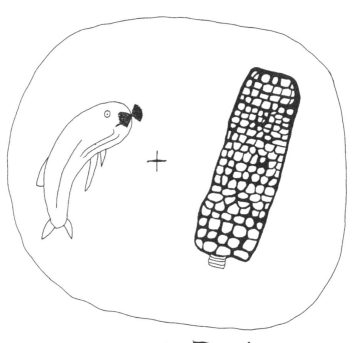

Difficult Dishes

Ambiguous Norway

Inhibited Mascot

The harpist at the sheraton.

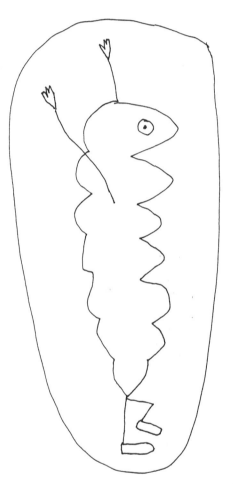

Dancing to the Thompson Twins

Ladie's Night

"Lemme get a better look at you, doll".

12:00 AM
11:00 PM
9:00 PM
7:00 PM

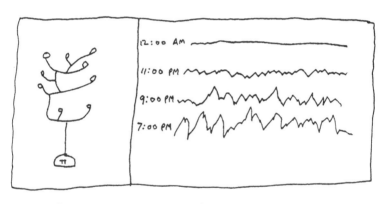

EKG ON A CANDLESTICK

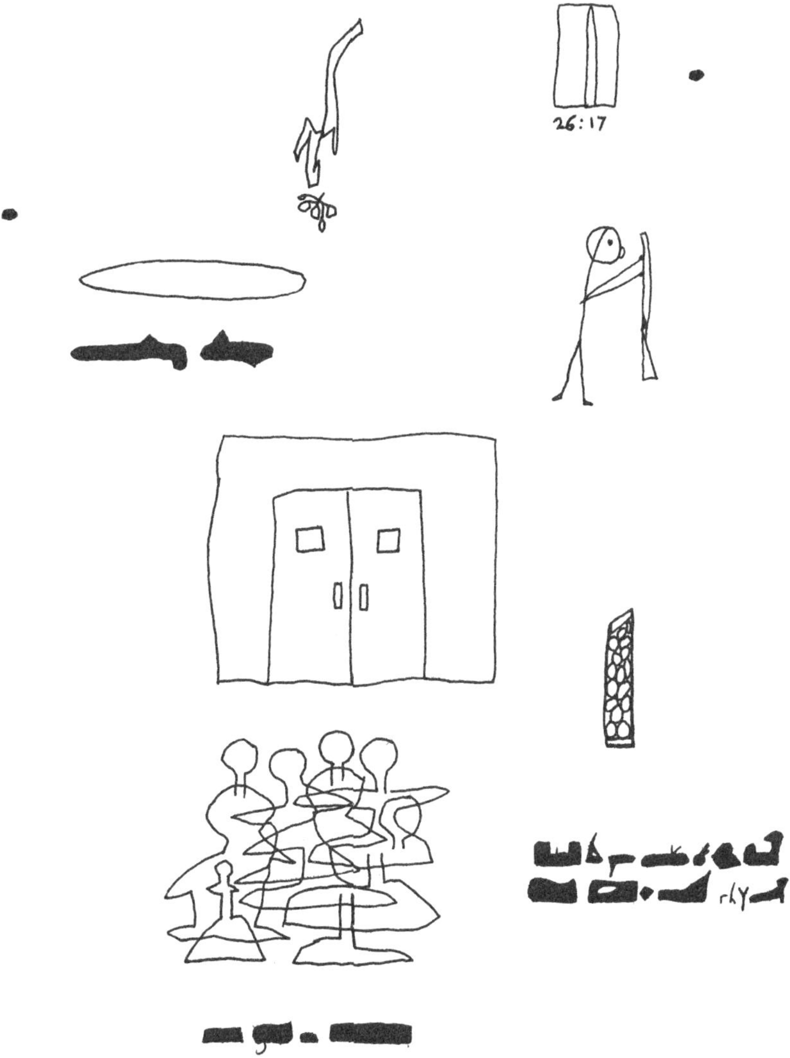
26:17

The Overthrow of Fine Dining

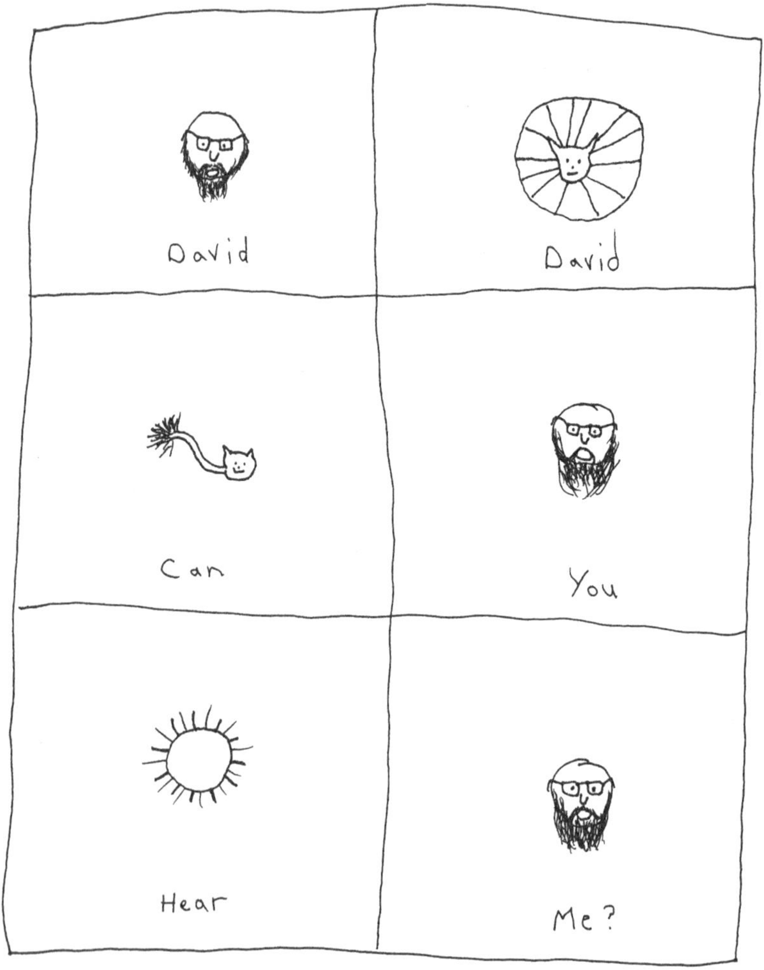
David
David
Can
You
Hear
Me?

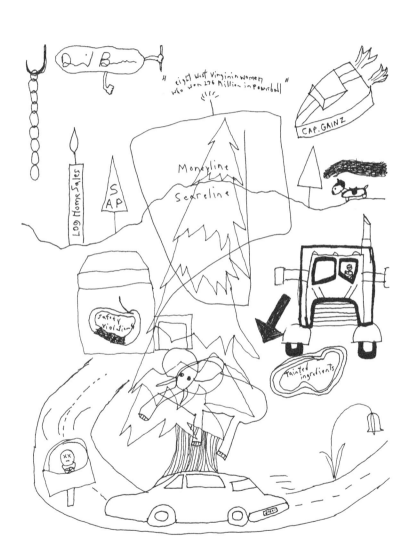

"eight West Virginia women who won 276 Million in powerball"

CAP.GAINZ

Log Home Sales

SAP

Moneyline
Scoreline

safety violation

tainted ingredients

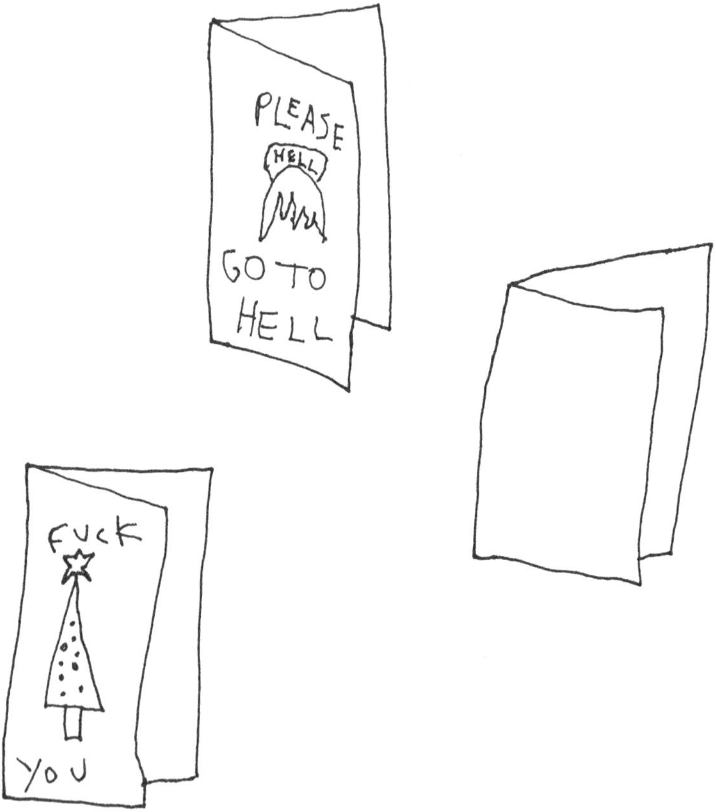
PLEASE
HELL
GO TO
HELL
FUCK
YOU

Braille Hoax

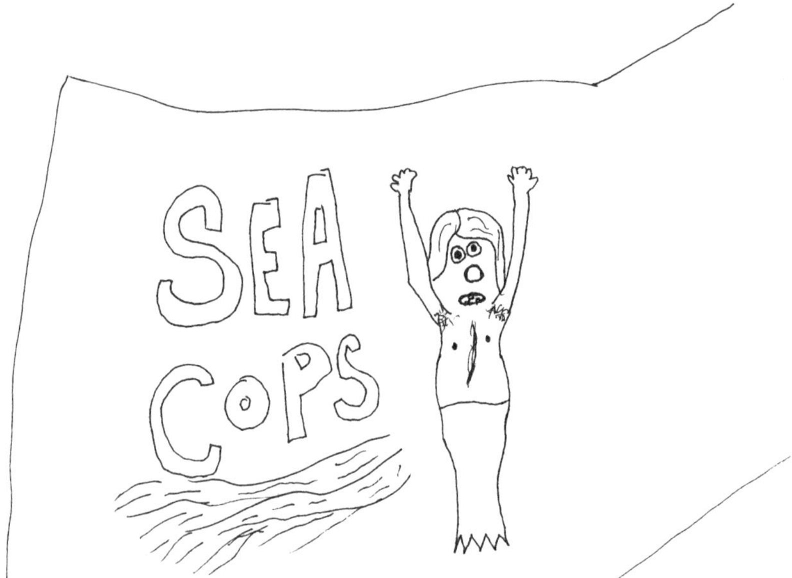
SEA
COPS

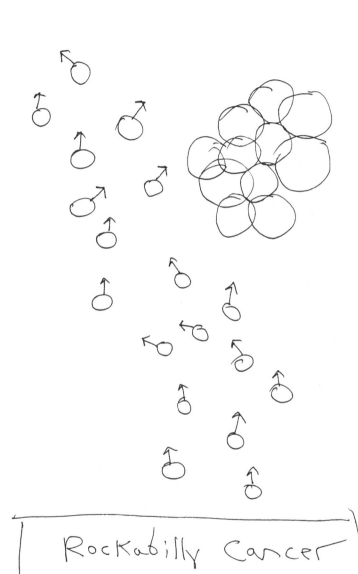

Rockabilly Cancer

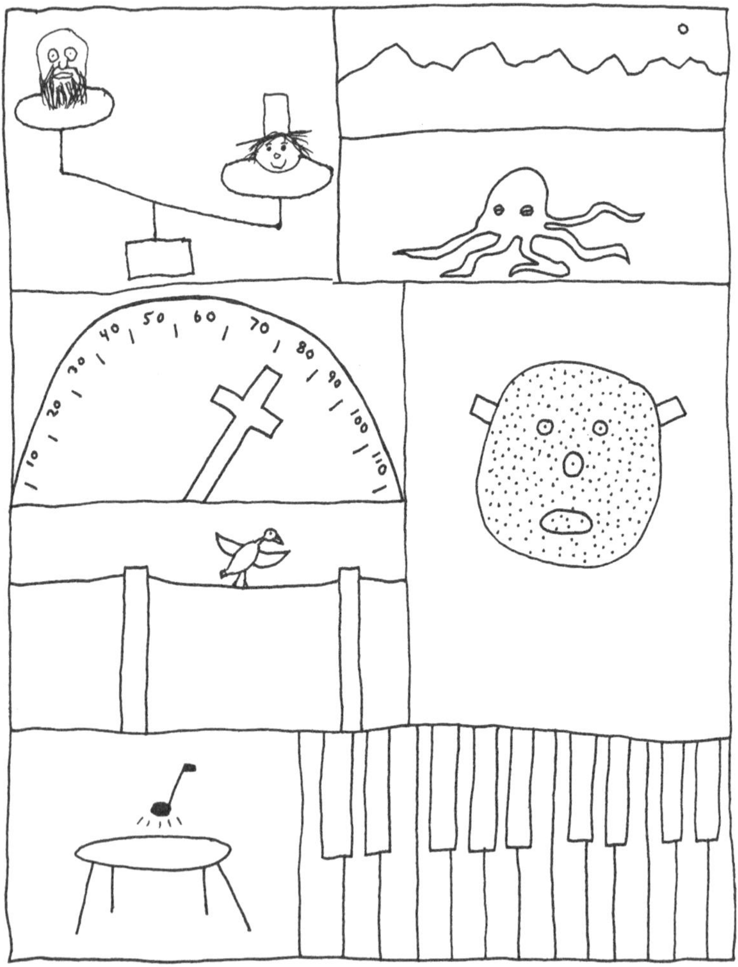
10 20 30 40 50 60 70 80 90 100 110

Hamburger Serenade

All Culture Strives,
Folks.

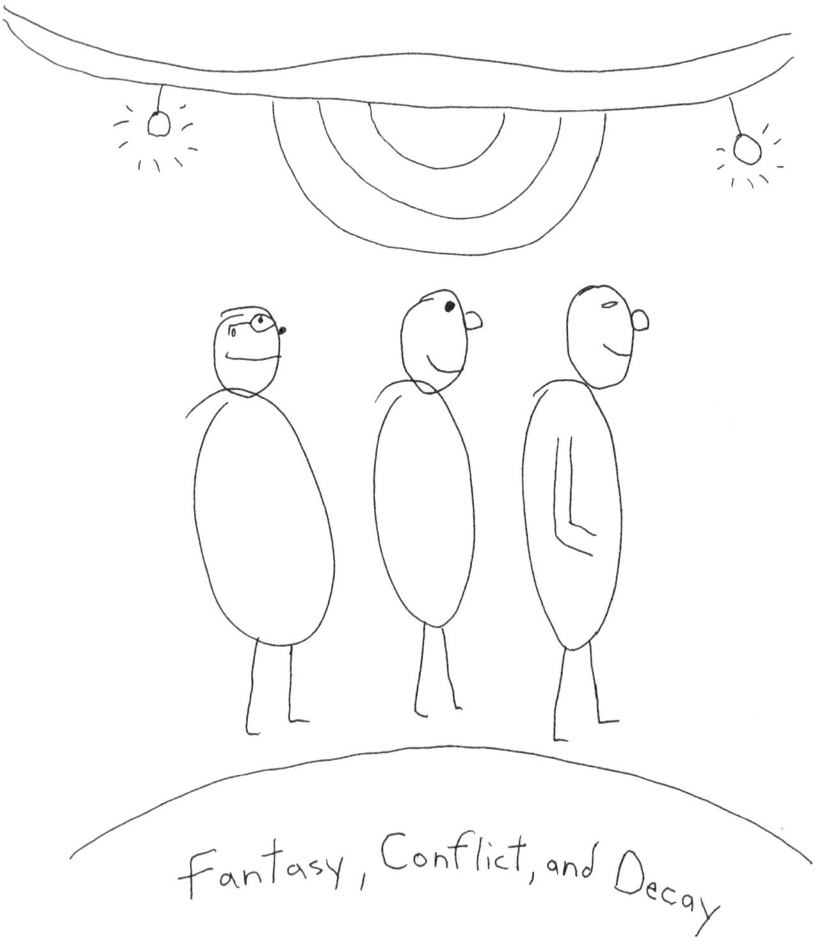
Fantasy, Conflict, and Decay

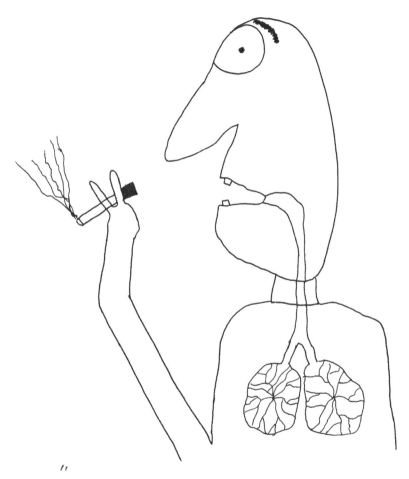

"I get a strange kind of pleasure
out of barely hanging on."

We start out
Life
Having Won
a Race.

Wind up
Humbled
by the Void.

LATE·LIFE REALIZATION

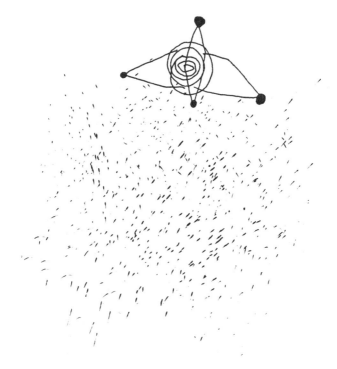

Modes of Night

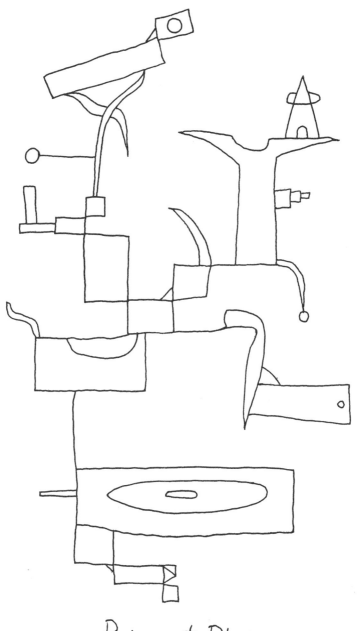

Poignant Play

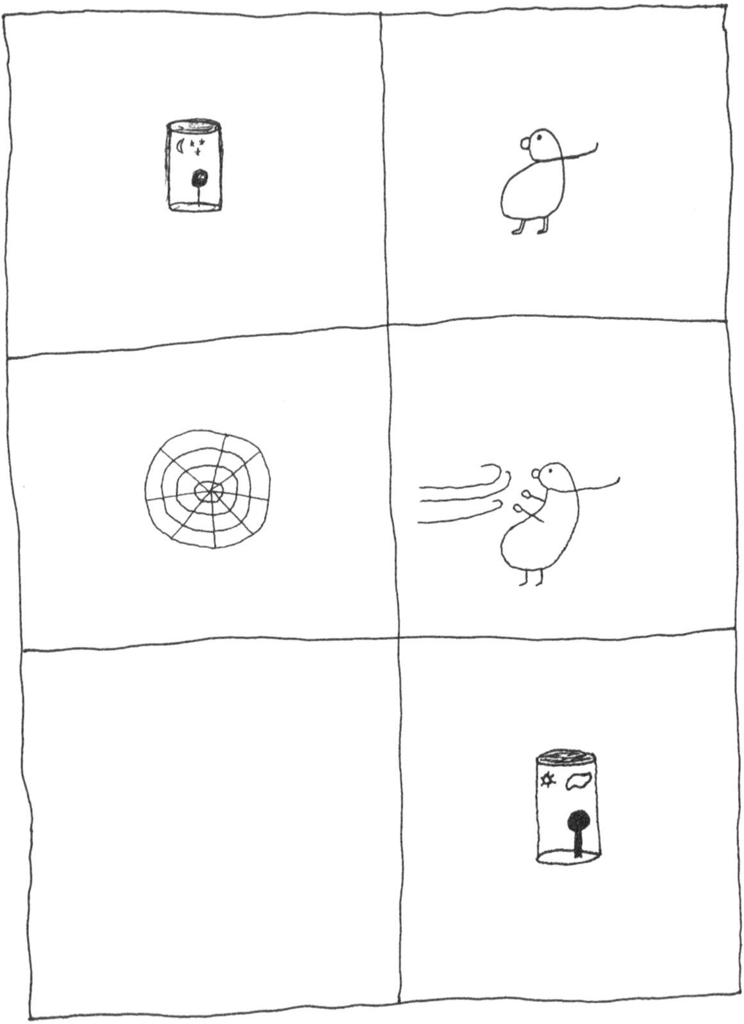

Find a Little Place

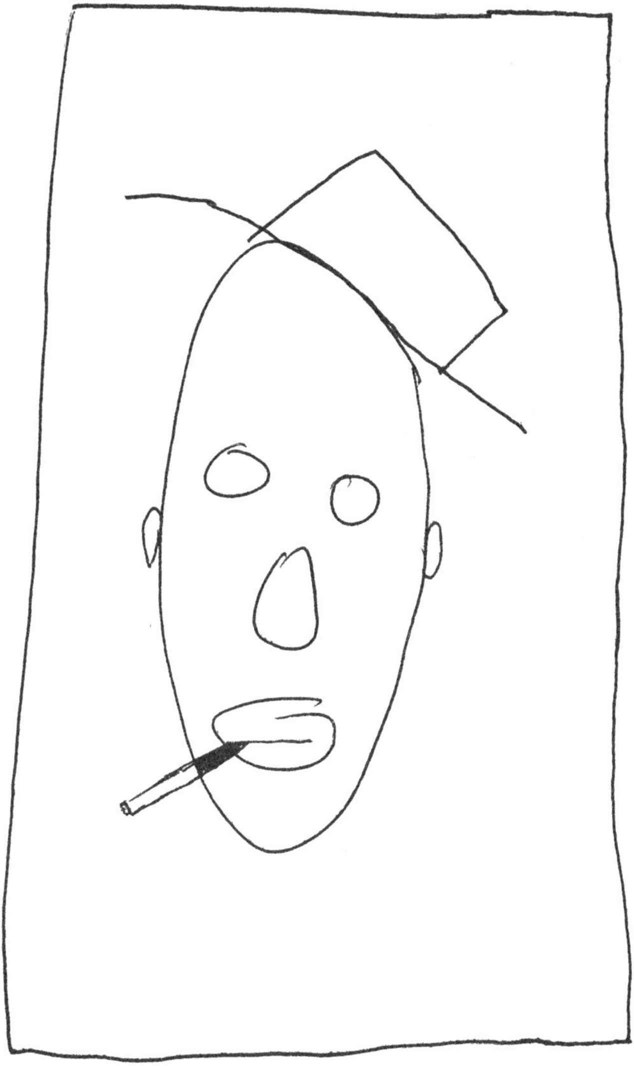

You're in trouble or you're not

Don't leave Death
                   a nice clean shot.

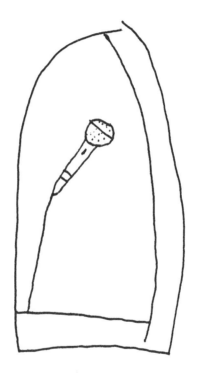

Demand this of thyself